DANCERCIZE

DANCERCIZE

by
Debbie Drake

Photographs by
Richard Hochman

Prentice-Hall, Inc., Englewood Cliffs, N.J.

DANCERCIZE
by Debbie Drake

Second printing...... February, 1970

Library of Congress Catalog Card Number: 67-16385

Printed in the United States of America

T 19668

Prentice-Hall International, Inc., London
Prentice-Hall of Australia, Pty. Ltd., Sydney
Prentice-Hall of Canada, Ltd., Toronto
Prentice-Hall of India Private Ltd., New Delhi
Prentice-Hall of Japan, Inc., Tokyo

This book is dedicated to that first primordial female creature who
upon catching a glimpse of herself in a quiet forest pool, knew
the first urge to adorn and enhance the image reflected
there—and to all of her sisters since who have kept
the spark of desire for personal beauty alive.

ACKNOWLEDGEMENTS

First and foremost, my sincere appreciation goes to Beverly Mosko, who helped give birth to an idea I conceived some years ago. Her invaluable assistance in helping me to create the movements for Dancercize have made this book possible. My thanks, also, to Kirk of International Dance Studio for his instruction in Oriental dance and for his help in planning photographs.

I would like to express my gratitude to Theo Eson, Marlene Fann and Char Blaisdell for their help in doing research and for their creative ideas; to Stephen Mosko and James Schwanke for the many hours spent in research for the chapter on culture; and to Nancy Terry for her assistance in assembling this book. Thanks, too, to Frank Wagner, Harry Wooliver and Bill Gary.

To my editor, Ann Pinchot, goes my appreciation for helping me to formulate many of my ideas. Many thanks to Nick D'Incecco, public relations director at Prentice-Hall, for his guidance.

Much of the material on nutrition was gathered with the help of the Honorable George Mehren, Assistant Secretary of the Department of Agriculture. He introduced me to people in the department and supplied my library with many interesting books and pamphets.

Several schools of dance have been very helpful: the Ballet Arts and Hope Moore Dance School in Denver, the June Taylor Dance School and Luigi Jazz Center and the International Dance School in New York.

My medical advisors are Dr. Lloyd Lundsten and Dr. Cary Whitacre. My breathing coach is Dr. Antonio Brico, noted symphony conductor.

Appreciation goes to Mr. Alfredo of Via Veneto for my hair styling.

And special credit goes to the renowned photographer, Richard Hochman.

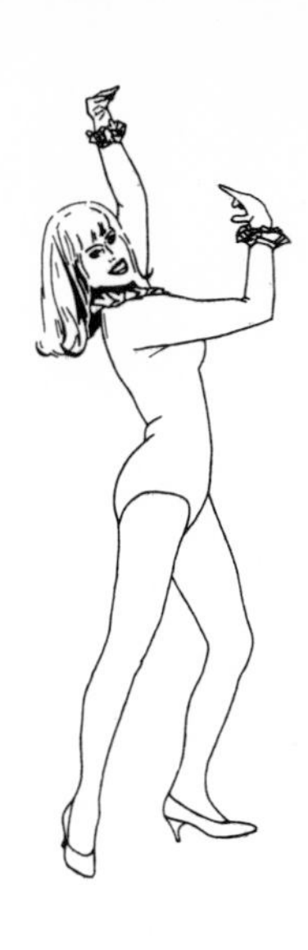

CONTENTS

1. SEXY OR SEXLESS? 13

2. PASSPORT TO BEAUTY AND HAPPINESS 19

3. YOUR MAGIC KEY—MENTAL DISCIPLINE 27

4. GOOD NUTRITION AND PROPER EATING HABITS EQUAL A SLIM WELL-PROPORTIONED FIGURE 31

5. BECOME A TANTALIZING FEMALE 48

6. SIX WEEKS TO A MORE BEAUTIFUL YOU 52

7. POLISHING THE PERSONALITY 168

8. BEAUTY IS MORE THAN A FIGURE AND FACE 173

9. THE ART OF LIVING 189

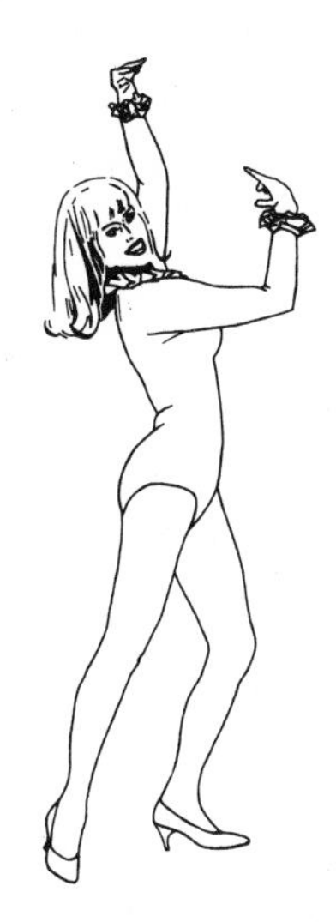

INTRODUCTION

A prerequisite for any book is a need for what that book has to offer. There has never been more of a need for a new system to guide you to *complete* beauty. Complete beauty includes the outward appearance as well as the inner person that radiates through.

I have on my library shelf a book on reducing that is over 100 years old. The exercises it gives are very similar to those given in many books today, and yet women are still struggling with the problem of unsightly bulges. What is needed is a new system of figure control; this you will find in the following pages.

A good figure is not the only factor in external beauty. A clear skin, shining hair, an air of well-being are also important. By following the methods outlined in this book, you will find that all these assets can be yours.

The second component for complete beauty deals with the mind. Can a woman really be beautiful, regardless of her proportions, if she is dull or stupid? The myth about "beautiful, but dumb" women being attractive to men has been exploded. In answer to the need for inner beauty, I have included in this book a chapter of culture. In reading it, I'm sure you will find the sense of "completeness" so necessary to a woman of today's world.

I offer this book to you as an extension of any former method you may have ever tried.

SEXY OR SEXLESS?

You who are now reading this book probably rank in the upper one-third of all women. You are attractive, intelligent and reasonably well liked, or at least have the potential for these attributes. I can assume this because you are reading this book, probably with self-improvement in mind. The other two-thirds will put off doing anything about their shortcomings with excuses like: "I'm too busy to take time to look better. Only vain and conceited women would spend that much time on their looks," or "There is really nothing I can do about how I look—some people are just born beautiful."

These women are invisible in today's society. The world passes them by without paying the least bit of attention to them. Movies, television and magazines bring to every man pictures of how beautiful women can be. Ask yourself how *you* compare! If you fall way below your best potential you had better watch out. A man likes to have pride in his woman—or he will find a woman of whom he can be proud.

The key word then is sex appeal.

The omnipotent process of sex, as it is woven into the texture of men's and women's bodies, is the pattern for the whole of life. Woman as the reproductive vessel is endowed by nature with special insights, charm and an integral responsibility to the future generations. These intangible characteristics are inherent in every female creature. Sex appeal, charm, desirability—call it what you will, it is an indispensable factor for women of any age. It is woman's greatest strength, just as strength is man's greatest charm. Maggie, in James Barrie's *What Every Woman Knows* wisely says, "It's sort of bloom on a woman. If you have it you don't need anything else."

Likewise, there is a lot of wisdom in Roland Young's lighthearted rhyme that says, ". . . and there's the happy bounding flea—You cannot tell the he from she—The sexes are alike you see; But she can tell and so can he!"

The important thing to know is that you CAN be a more attractive and desirable woman. There is no reason why a smart girl need play second fiddle to a golf course or a sports car. A little attention to detail, and that handsome, girl-shy hunk of male in the engineering department could suddenly discover that you would look a lot better in the right-hand seat of his Porsche than even his beloved golf clubs. And try not to act too surprised if the junior executive in the inner office should walk up and ask you out to lunch.

These things have happened. But they happen to smart girls who know the importance of details. Often a thing as slight as a change in your eyeliner can make your eyes look twice as large. A weight loss of only three pounds can make you look as good going as you do coming. And if you are married, your body and your looks are every bit as important to your happiness as if you were single.

With the best intentions in the world, a husband has been conditioned, by the times, to expect his wife to wear many hats—sweetheart, wife, housekeeper, companion, hostess and mother to his children. But husbands too are human! A good looking wife is a boost to their male egos, saying in effect, "Look at the gal *I* was able to snare."

Then too, by keeping your body young and alive, you will maintain better health. You will be better able to handle your daily problems as they arise. For a double bonus you will have the happiest, proudest husband in the neighborhood.

With all of these wonderful rewards what are you waiting for? Surely there is no better way to spend your time than working toward these goals. For in spite of what you may hear to the contrary, happiness is a trim, healthy and sexy body!

When I was a scrawny, self-conscious teenager in Dallas, I began buying all of the beauty hints and exercise magazines I could find. My figure then was a carpenter's dream—straight up and down. My kind and helpful friends went out of their way to tell me that since that was the way I was built there was little that could be done about it.

It seemed grossly unfair that I should be stuck with an ugly body and have nothing that I could do about it. So I exercised anyway. I knew I had a long way to go and a lot of things to change, but I was willing to gamble. Within a few months, I had proved to my delight that I could have curves, but in the process I had begun overeating and ended up with a surplus of curves!

This required dieting and exercising to slim my body. When I finally reached my ideal proportions, I had seen the figure problems from both sides of the fence—underweight and overweight—and I knew the horrible feelings that went with both. Happily, I also knew that each problem could be corrected, and how to correct it.

The idea of anyone going through life with the social and psychological handicap of a sexless figure was the worst thing I could imagine. So I established reducing salons to help women find their way to a beautiful body. Here all my exercises were tested and retested to find which were most effective, the best way to do each one and how much could be expected from each.

From there I went to TV and then to books, always showing how a person who cares about her looks can achieve miracles, simply with motivation and hard work.

When I said hard work, I meant just that—HARD WORK.

It doesn't seem like it should be asking too much of a woman to spend 15 to 30 minutes a day doing exercises that will give her a sexy, enchanting body for the other 1,425 minutes that are left. But for some reason, many women find exercising boring and a drudge. Even I, knowing how vitally important exercises are, would sometimes find myself wanting to skip now and then. But the key to exercise is in doing them every single—don't you dare miss even one—day.

What a drag! And yet they work so well. What is a girl to do? There must be an easier way. . . .

And there is—DANCERCIZE.

When I first found the answer, I was dubious. Dancercize was so much fun, I wondered if it could possibly be as good for you as the harder, conventional exercises. I tested it in clinics and on television and was delighted to discover that it works *even better* than calisthenic-type exercises.

Dancercize not only remolds your body, but gives you grace, poise and beauty. It is fun and it makes you look, act and feel twice as pretty. Men are quick to notice the difference. There is nothing so irresistible and enticing to them as the panther-like grace that comes only from the coordination learned from the dance. Feminine body movements should be fluid—never stiff, never awkward, never inhibited. Dancercize enables a woman to relax, to loosen up, to carry herself tall and proudly, to be in command of things at all times and to gain confidence and poise.

Helen Gurley Brown, author of the well-known *Sex and the Single Girl*, and editor of *Cosmopolitan* magazine says frankly: "The art of making love is probably the epitome of self-expression. The art of dancing is a somewhat less intense form of self-expression, but also rewarding. The two arts are not dissimilar it seems to me. . . . When you dance you feel womanly, sexy, like a creature of nature. . . . the exact opposite of being inhibited. Dancing has allowed a lot of girls to express themselves physically so that they can go out and become better love mates than if there had never been dancing in their lives."

Many women, when they first start Dancercizing, are apt to be awkward and self-conscious. When they are supposed to stretch their arms out wide, they only do it about halfway. They tend to keep the elbows bent and their arms in, close to their bodies. Their beginning movements are usually tiny, shy ones, and they are tense and ill at ease with the music. After just a few months I would find their arms stretching way out. With new confidence, their movements would become more spontaneous and graceful. They were fully in control of their bodies, moving as they wanted to. They could dance proudly, with their heads high and their motions assured.

Happily, I noticed that this magic effect did not end when they stopped dancing. It carried over into everything they did. Once a woman learns to move rhythmically, nothing can stop her. She can walk across a room in a way that is more interesting to men than someone else's low neckline. She can waltz or do the frug in a way that will turn others green with envy. She can outshine other competition just by standing or sitting, because Dancercize will give her the security of confidence, and there is nothing more attractive, more enticing to men than a confident, composed woman.

Every woman, regardless of age, wants to be all woman. She wants to feel that she is something special and unique. To feel dull and sexless is worse than suicide, it makes you a walking corpse. Every normal woman wants to feel that she is attractive to look at and fun to be with. I know the feeling. This book was written because a homely little 15-year-old wanted more than anything else in the world to feel that she was a woman—to feel desirable, alive and vibrant. It was written because she refused to settle for a second-class ticket through life.

Life is relatively short and its moments are precious. Any woman would be a fool to settle for less than all of the wonderful things life has to offer her.

Take a good look around you. Your world is like a rare flower waiting to bloom, but a flower cannot bloom until its environment is right. Likewise, you will remain an outsider, shut off from the stream of life until your attitudes become those which will encourage the bud to bloom.

Absorb this book. Within these pages you will find a whole new way of life. With a little time and effort this new and exciting, completely feminine world that you deserve can be yours. But remember it will do you no good whatsoever just to read the book and agree with what it says. Only one thing can whisk you away from a sexless body and a dull life. Only one thing can start you on that promised path to a richer and fuller life. Action. To read, to understand, is not enough, you must act on what you learn.

Following is a chart. Here you can rate yourself in just about everything you desire. This will help you to better understand what you have and what you need. Define your disaster areas. Throughout the book you will find answers to all of your problems. Check the areas where you need help and then read on to find it!

FIGURE CHECKLIST

FACE:	Firming o	Clearing up o	
CHIN:	Reducing o	Firming o	
NECK:	Tightening o	Smoothing o	
POSTURE:	Overall correction o	Aligning certain areas o	
SHOULDERS:	Slimming o	Building up o	
UPPER ARMS:	Losing o	Gaining o	Firming o
TUMMY:	Losing o	Firming o	
BACK:	Losing o	Gaining o	Strengthening o
HIPS:	Losing o	Gaining o	Reshaping o
THIGHS:	Losing o	Gaining o	Firming o
CALVES:	Losing o	Gaining o	Shaping o
ANKLES:	Losing o		
HANDS:	Improved circulation o	Achieve grace o	
MIDRIFF:	Losing o	Firming o	
WAIST:	Losing o	Firming o	
BOSOM:	Gaining o	Losing o	Firming o

PASSPORT TO BEAUTY AND HAPPINESS

In this book I want to give women all over the world the newest, most enjoyable and easiest ways to have a slim figure and at the same time feel more womanly. Even more important I want this book to be the key to transforming your body *and* your mind, to changing your whole concept of living into a new way of life.

This new book should be used like a handbook or encyclopedia of beauty knowledge, to answer your every question (whether you are mature or a teen-ager) about how to become the beautiful, whole and wholesome creature that our Creator intended you to be.

Like many women, with the best intentions, you may have started on reducing programs and followed them enthusiastically for a few weeks or months and then have digressed and slipped back into the old CARELESS ways. After studying my new book you will be motivated to a higher degree, you will have a better understanding of why your efforts in the past failed, and you will know what to do to insure success.

The magic key to success in any effort is *MOTIVATION*. Unless we are goaded in our desires by an intense motivation, there is rarely any accomplishment. What I am going to do in this book is to show you how to develop a motivation. There are a million people in this world, each with a different key or motivation. I can't give you a tangible key that will unlock secret knowledge, but I can show you how you can find your own key.

I can show you how other people have found their way to going on a reducing plan and how their motivational key has helped them develop the willpower to stick to it. Without the discipline of willpower we can accomplish nothing physically, so the first step in this book will be to help you find a way to develop stick-to-itiveness. Unless you are really determined to find and maintain your own perfect figure, it would be a waste of time to even start on the Dancercize Program. Believe me, it would be distressing to me to know that you had been unable to maintain your goal once you had found it.

The first thing, of course, will be to establish what your personal, perfect figure should be; what you should weigh and measure, taking into account your basic body structure, height, etc.

Next, and even more important, you must make your own complete analysis. Not just of your weight, size and height, but a complete personality checklist about *you,* your interests, your beliefs, even your problems. How well do you like yourself? How do you compete in the world of culture? What do you know about art and painting, the theater, the world's literature? Are you poised and comfortable among educated people? Are you tongue-tied and ill at ease in a conversation about world problems, political issues or the latest book or play?

Today, even the Miss Universe contestants, admittedly the world's exponents of physical beauty, must display their talents as well as their measurements. They must prove that they are not just idle ornaments to society. Personality, ability and intelligence weigh as much or more with the judges, than do their physical attributes.

Farther along in the book you will find a checklist to help you analyze your failures in the past. For instance, have you ever gone to a reducing salon? Have you exercised with someone on TV? How many diets have you gone on in the past? Have they been successful, or have they all failed? How long did you stay with any plan?

You must ask yourself these questions to get an idea of the kind of self-discipline you have, the problems you have had in the past and what it will take to conquer them. In the chapter on Willpower we intend to show you how to do this very thing—conquer your past problems, no matter what they have been.

The first thing we are going to do is create a brand-new self-image for you. It will be just like taking all your old mental clothing out of the closet and then starting to carefully select brand-new becoming attire.

I want you to learn to like yourself for what you are. I want to show you how to change your attitudes and thoughts, as well as your physical appearance. I am convinced that what each one of us wants is more life! When we experience happiness, self-confidence, success, we enjoy more life. When we allow ourselves to suffer anxiety, self-doubt and otherwise inhibit our God-given abilities and talents, we literally turn our backs on the gift our Creator has given us.

When your self-image is to your liking, you feel good. When it is threatened you feel insecure, anxious, ill at ease. When you feel adequate, your confidence shows in wholesome pride. You feel free to "be yourself", to express yourself. When you subconsciously dislike or are ashamed of yourself you want to hide. If your creative sense is stifled, you may even become hostile and hard to get along with.

Fortunately, psychologists have discovered that we are all endowed with a self-help mechanism that is built into our minds and hearts by our Creator. All we have to do is to learn how to let it function in our behalf.

This mysterious "something" works like a modern electronic data processing computer. If we feed our subconscious data-bank with only the information that we are inferior, dull, incapable clods, unfortunately, that is just what we will be.

First you are going to learn to like yourself no matter how hopeless and frustrated you may feel. I want you to stop dramatizing yourself as an object of pity and despair. Stop carrying around a mental picture of yourself as a defeated, hopeless case.

Your program for getting more living out of life will include learning how to put this wonderful built-in creative force to work for you. The method will consist of learning, practicing and experiencing. It will mean establishing new habits of thinking, imagining, remembering and acting to bring about the personality you were created to be, for remember, "As a man thinketh so he is."

Many people shy away from self-acceptance because they insist on identifying themselves with their past mistakes. Well, we all make mistakes, but our mistakes do not necessarily have to make us!

You wouldn't dream of throwing away a typewriter because it made a typographical error, but many of us feel that it is hopeless to try to diet or improve our figure because we have failed in one or two attempts in the past.

However, it is only intelligent to learn to recognize our mistakes and shortcomings before we can hope to correct them. So start off by accepting yourself for what you are and then go from there. Learn to *tolerate and understand the causes* of your imperfections *rather than hate yourself because of them.*

Now that you have decided to sculpt a new body more to your liking, you will find it necessary to do a little pruning on some of your old and CARELESS habits too.

I want you to get to know the joy of being feminine. (Remember the delightful number from the musical, "Flower Drum Song," when Suzie Wong sings, "I Enjoy Being A Girl"?) Women were created with special female wiles to delight the male. If you don't believe it, watch how a father responds to a small daughter as soon as she is old enough to ply her charms on him. Unfortunately, too many women do everything they can to destroy the image of femininity. They neglect their hair and skin, wear sloppy slacks, go out in public with hair in curlers—worse yet, they greet their husbands that way when they come home from work. The contrast must be painfully evident to a man who has been exposed all day to the chic, intelligent and vital gals who compose the business girls' world.

This is where much of the early emphasis of this book will be expended. To be successful you must be consistent. It is not conducive to seeing results if you progress one day and slide back the next.

Keep a calendar and keep a record. Always plan ahead for the next day and then stick to it. Don't let yourself fall back on the alibi that you do not have time. Consult your record and see how much time you have let the telephone consume in idle chatter.

Interest your children in your new project. You will find to your pleasure that they will probably enjoy doing the Dancercizes with you, and will join with a natural abandon that you would do well to emulate. Delegate more small tasks and responsibilities to them. You will gain two-fold—more time for yourself and character-building responsibility for the children.

Mind is the strongest part of the body. Tell yourself over and over what it is you want! Where there is no desire, there is no accomplishment. Do not accept excuses from yourself. A tiny roll of fat around your waistline will not go away by itself. Let it be a warning that little rolls of fat have a way of becoming bulges that are hard to take off.

Try to think of new ways to help you stick to your plan once you have started on your Dancercize goal. Plan wholesome meals for your family.

Make menus ahead and stick to them, shopping with your menus in mind so that you will not fall back on the excuse that you will have to settle for a less balanced meal because you do not have time to run to the store today.

Deliberately eliminate desserts from your meals. No one in the family will miss them if you have served a good, nourishing meal. Desserts are not really healthy and should NEVER BE SERVED AS PART OF THE MEAL.

DON'T KEEP SWEETS IN THE HOUSE AS A TEMPTATION. If you have a sweet tooth, developed more than likely from poor eating habits, try keeping a bowl of fresh fruit or high protein snacks around to allay your desire.

Try not to miss one day once you have embarked on your plan. (You will find that Sundays are the worst days for backsliding because of our living patterns.) If you do slip, try to plan a more disciplined next week. DON'T GET DISCOURAGED.

Keep your goals modest at first. Build up with time. Remind yourself that if you gain nothing more than improved health and vitality you will be miles ahead toward happiness.

Remember too that group therapy is good. Be a leader and interest the Kaffee-Klatsch friends in joining your plan to improve your mind and body. Turn the doughnuts and coffee hour into a discussion group over issues raised in last night's newspaper or the current issue of *World News* or *Time* magazine.

Don't be like the heroine described in *Sabrina Has a Thousand Charms:*

> Her eyes are as cupid's arms, her smile a golden chain
> But when the beauteous idiot speaks, her tongue
> My spellbound fetters break
> And I, her slave, am free again.

Let us get back to the basic premise of this book—Dancercize. Our Creator designed our bodies to function at their highest potential through activity. But in this electronic age of pushbuttons and robot-like machines, our physical life gets easier and easier. Counselors, who deal with the problems of living stress today, know that there is no better way to relieve tension and anxiety than to move. (Have you ever tried to worry sitting still? Your instinct is to pace the floor, is it not?)

When you let your body fall into the graceful forms of the dance that music calls forth instinctively, you not only exercise and tighten your muscles, but you get an extra bonus in grace and a feeling of internal loveliness for your effort. It is a well-known fact that no woman is truly beautiful unless she feels beautiful.

Before you say you can't dance, remember that all children are born with an inherent sense of rhythm. It is only the inhibitions and disciplines of our adult society that stultifies that sense. So don't become discouraged or become irritable with yourself if grace doesn't come instantly. There are many checkmates that will keep you from grace at first. Two of the worst offenders are fatigue and tension. This is where your basic mental conditioning will again come to your rescue, for without it exercise, diet, and grooming would be of little worth.

Dancing is one of the most primitive forms of expression known to man. Even the most primitive tribes of aborigines performed some form of rhythmic dance, often using it as a form of pagan worship and thanksgiving. Dancing is the epitome of self-expression among the art forms since it translates life itself.

Thus, when you dance you feel womanly, feminine and sexy—like a creature of nature. Latins, who are noted for being sexy, always seem to be naturally dancing and enjoying themselves. Puritans, on the other hand, were strictly denied this form of enjoyment.

A famous doctor, who specializes in psychosomatic medicine, advises his tension patients to put records on the phonograph and just move to the music. Try it. It doesn't matter how silly your movements are. Do anything you want or that the music tells you to do. You can try to imitate the pretty chorus girls, the graceful ballerina or even the wildly flirting movements of the discotheque dancers on TV. The important thing is that you are releasing the tensions in your body. You are giving your muscles play, and at the same time you are relieving the frustrations deep within your subconscious that cry out for attention. Later in the book we will go into the matter of controlled Dancercize and the methods for getting the most good from it.

You will find right from the start that the new Dancercize method of exercise will make you feel more womanly. When you look into a mirror you will feel feminine and pretty.

Conventional exercise, while it is stimulating, fails completely to make you feel glamorous. It also fails in providing the added benefits of coordination. With Dancercize, the reward is coordination and memory—mental effort that stimulates the mind as well as the muscles.

There is no age limit to women's need for beauty. I have had women in my classes as old as seventy years and as young as fourteen. All had different problems, goals or reasons for wanting to obtain a more perfect figure.

There was the teenager who had never known what it was to be popular because of her obesity problem. She had developed such a complex that she was near to withdrawing from reality altogether. Strangely, her problem was enlarged because in her unhappy state she sought solace in "goodies" that merely compounded her problem.

After she started losing weight she discovered that she was also gaining a better complexion because of her wholesome diet.

A completely new world was opened to her, one that she had hoped to know. She found the joy of popularity among new friends and even had dates, being asked out with the "gang" to sock hops and other school functions.

There was also the young married woman who was trying to cope with marital unhappiness—not due necessarily to her husband's inadequacies and quarrels, but largely because she didn't like herself. Much of the time she did not feel well. She lacked energy, which made her a poor wife and a cross, cantankerous mother.

But after she had embarked on this new project and she began to feel more grace in her movements and to see visible evidence of inches coming off in the right places, she began to realize that it wasn't her home life that she had been dissatisfied with as much as it was her heavy hips and thighs.

She suddenly found to her delight that her children didn't annoy her so much. She even found that her husband was much nicer to her (probably because it *is* easier to be nice to a pretty person).

Suddenly she found that instead of feeling that life had passed her by, she was developing a whole new set of interests and a better figure than she had known even as a teenager (probably because she had never before tried an exercise program). She learned at that late date that often a person can be physically active and still have a thick waistline.

These are just a few examples of the dramatic experiences that have resulted from my new Dancercize method that has been tested and proved in our clinics all over the world. At some of our figure clinics I have seen girls go from a size sixteen to a size thirteen in two weeks, and from a size fourteen to a size twelve with as much as eighteen pounds in weight loss.

In general I do not recommend this much weight loss over a short period of time, but in some cases I have found it good since such dramatic results often help to spur women on to higher goals. Once started, women generally will stick to this method because of the added bonus benefits of health, poise and confidence, as well as good looks.

In this book no part of the anatomy is overlooked. There is an exercise designed to trim or resculpture almost any section of the physical frame. I want to give you a shapely and beautiful figure first of all, but with an added bonus of better health and more natural energy with which to enjoy your new-found life. Beauty without health would be incomplete.

You must realize from the beginning that this is not a temporary program—you are embarking on a whole new way of life. You are going to look at food differently; at exercise differently because it is in a new and more digestible form. The benefits you are going to receive—*and the fun*—will lift you out of the dull "everydayness" of your past routines.

The hour you spend (or even 30 minutes) will lift you to unbelievable heights of stimulation. Your time for daily Dancercize will become your happiest hour. It will become your escape from all the unpleasant things in the past and will lift you into a mood of complete and exultant happiness. You will find that happiness is an important factor in this book. It is woman's right and nature to be happy. We think better, feel better, our senses are keener and we are even healthier when we are happy.

I would like to suggest the purchase of a full-length mirror to hang in a strategic place in the room where you will be doing your dancercizes so that you can have a full view of the transformation that will be taking place in you. I want you to check yourself at the end of three weeks of consistent Dancercize against the person you were at the beginning of the first week. Do not be discouraged if nothing drastic seems to be happening. Reserve your judgment for at least 21 days. By then you will have shown dramatic improvement.

YOUR MAGIC KEY —MENTAL DISCIPLINE

Tired of that old "five-by-five" bit? Have you decided to sculpture a new figure more to your liking? Welcome to the club! It may be comforting to know that at some time in their lives more than three-fourths of the women in the world have felt dissatisfaction with their natural endowments and have wished they could change them. Many have even embarked on the road toward making themselves over into a more pleasing image, but too many of them have been flagged down on their initial trip by complete and frustrating failure.

WHY?

We know that nothing succeeds like success. Failure begets failure. But I cannot believe that any normal person would rather be overweight, dull and unkempt, than slender, vibrant and full of the joy of living.

I can only believe that their indifference stems from a hurt or injury to their ego in the past. Perhaps a lack of popularity as a youth, coupled with a husband's growing indifference or cooling ardor has brought to the surface old fears, old scars, old failures.

Let's go back to your personality chart and see if we can uncover your motivation. (For unless you are truly motivated by a deep desire to create a new and more pleasing self-image, you are wasting your time to even read any farther.)

Still with me? Good!

Who are you? A married woman? Perhaps one with a growing family that consumes too much of your time and energy? An office career gal in a physical and mental rut? An older woman whose family is suddenly grown and gone, leaving an empty void and a useless, life-gone-by feeling? Or are you a teen-ager who wants to latch on to the lovely merry-go-round of living but feels inadequate, awkward and not as pretty as the other girls?

Let's start off with the basic premise of this book. Every human being was meant by his Creator to be a happy, creative individual—"You." Not a carbon copy of every other person, but a unique bundle of genes unlike any other bundle of genes in this world. This is your own priceless birthright, but it is how you value it and what you make of it that counts.

A human being always acts and feels exactly the way he imagines himself to be. This is the basic law of the mind. It is the way we are built.

In terms of modern knowledge it is as if we are governed by a computer; a mechanism that gathers all of the information that is fed to it and comes up with answers that govern our daily lives. Therefore if we feed the governor nothing but negative, unhappy pictures of our self-image, it stands to reason that we will be negative, unhappy creatures.

This is not just supposition, but laboratory fact. Experiments with human behavior have proved that a person hypnotized in a warm room, when told that he is in the Arctic and freezing, will actually shudder from cold and his body will produce goose bumps. Others have even raised their temperature just by "imagining" themselves on the desert, suffering from heat and lack of water.

This is because the mind believes what it has been told and has in turn convinced the body.

So, why not imagine yourself slim, graceful, witty and charming? Isn't this what you really want to be?

Mental pictures offer us an opportunity to "practice" new traits and attitudes. It opens a new psychologic door since your nervous system cannot tell the difference between an actual experience and one that is vividly imagined. So, mentally "see" yourself as you would like to be. And remember! Practicing in your imagination will make for actual perfection!

But here I must warn you that passive wishing is not enough. To be powerful enough to change your negative beliefs about yourself and to change your whole behavior pattern, your thoughts must be rooted in DEEP DESIRE.

Create for yourself a new image. That is not to say an impossible image, however. Be realistic. You must know that you cannot change the bone structure of your body. You can redistribute the flesh, firm muscles to a more streamlined effect, remove excess pounds, but you cannot become short if you are tall, or petite if you have a large bone structure.

This is what we mean when we say, "Learn to like yourself first of all for what you are and then go on from there."

Think about your acquaintances. Surely there must be at least one person you know whom you admire greatly, whose body proportions or even facial features would not get them to tenth place in a beauty contest, but who carry themselves with an air of graceful confidence. Their very presence in a room creates an air of exuberance and their absence is felt at once when they leave.

Picture the kind of person you really want to be. Dwell on the idea and enumerate minute details of behavior. Select all of the desirable traits you admire in others and set yourself a definite goal. Be persistent in believing that this is truly what you want.

Remember that your self-image and your habits tend to go together. Change one and you will automatically change the other. Psychologists' tests have proved that more than two-thirds of our behavior, feelings and responses are based on habit. So let's set out to break our old, undesirable habits by substituting new and happier ones.

First and foremost will be your diet habits. Once you have started on the Dancercize and Beauty diet you will have a whole new concept of food. Food will not only be hunger-appeasing, but energy fuel as well. You will no longer be eating for the dubious "pleasure" of eating, but from natural appetite stimulated by your new-found activity. And this is where a double bonus comes in. The food you will be eating will give you new-found vigor and a greater desire for activity. Natural, eager activity, in turn, will automatically help to slim and trim your proportions.

Next, I want you to tell yourself that beginning today you are going to be more cheerful. Act friendlier (and what is more important), *Feel* friendlier toward those about you. Try to be less critical of other people and what you regard as their faults, failings and mistakes. Try to be conscious of your new personality and act as if it were true. Try to be optimistic and close your mind to negative thoughts.

I want you to consciously smile at least three times each day, and no matter what happens to upset you, grit your teeth and react calmly.

Remember, we are going to take one step at a time. Like the grains of sand in an hourglass slipping from one compartment to another, we can only do one thing at a time. So shut out of your mind all of the frustrating barriers that come with thinking about the "long road to success" that may lie ahead.

Realize that the jittery feelings that will attack you from time to time will come not from the work involved, but from your own attitudes. Keep telling yourself that you do not have to accomplish this overnight. Just concentrate on getting started. Then go on from there, one step at a time, in a completely relaxed and receptive mood.

Do not be so concerned or anxious about the end results that you try forcing results. For instance, don't "jam" your mental image by rushing out to buy a new and extreme style dress that you saw last week and that you would give a mint to be able to wear. Be wise and wait until the slack in your present dresses PROVES that you are ready for a change.

Just set the dress as a GOAL and then concentrate for awhile on skin care, manicures, pedicures. Experiment with new hair styles. Read a new book, go out and wish-shop—not necessarily to buy, but to discover some of the new and exciting gadgets that are being produced today to make life easier and more fun.

In other words, open up new horizons—stretch your mental muscles as well as those of your body!

Thus freed from anxiety and hurry, you will be able to concentrate on each step in orderly sequence. In this relaxed frame of mind you will probably be surprised at how quickly you will become aware of visible results.

Don't be afraid of mistakes. Let each mistake be a stepping stone to success. Recognize each mistake for what it is, then go forward, because we only learn by correcting. Skill of any kind is only attained by trial and error. There would be no great musicians, artists or dancers if they were to quit because of a few wrong notes, brush strokes or dance steps.

Think always in terms of the end results. Forget your past errors. Remember only the pleasure you are going to know when you have achieved your goal. Always keep the mental picture of yourself as you would like to be in the forefront.

Let your desire WORK FOR YOU NATURALLY rather than trying to FORCE IT TO WORK for you. Do not be too demanding of yourself. Remember what Alcoholics Anonymous teaches? "Don't try to quit drinking forever—only for today!"

Trust yourself, for it is deep inside yourself that the miracle will take place. You cannot wait until you see results before you begin to believe. You must act each minute, each day as if it were working—FOR THIS IS THE MAGIC KEY. ONLY IF YOU DO THIS WILL IT WORK.

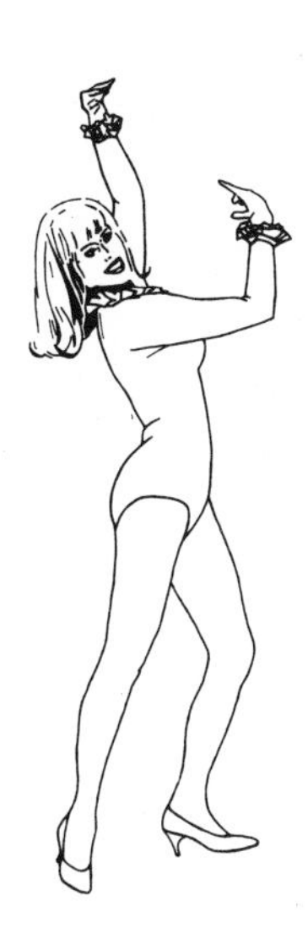

GOOD NUTRITION AND PROPER EATING HABITS EQUAL A SLIM WELL-PROPORTIONED FIGURE

Can better nutrition and proper eating habits help to slim you, proportion your figure, give a clearer skin, improve your energy and nerves, give you better vision, insure you more days bursting with health and vigor? The answer is definitely Yes. You may be both overweight and undernourished. You are less likely to have the habitual craving for excess food with a diet that supplies your body with its nutritional needs. When you learn how to select your foods and prepare them properly, you may find your intake of calories cut in half, and at the same time gain in nutritional value.

WHAT DO EATING HABITS AND NUTRITION HAVE TO DO WITH THE SHAPE OF YOUR FIGURE?

Being the correct weight is not satisfying enough if your figure is not well-proportioned. Good eating habits may not increase a size A to a B cup, but they will decrease those oversize D cups. The way you eat can help give you flatter, more youthful hips. That protruding tummy you thought was here to stay can disappear. You need only to understand and apply a few sensible rules. Chances are that your present eating habits were not formed with the idea of sculpturing your figure to perfection. Neither were they designed to give you that extra vitality and health that should rightfully be yours.

You may be surviving on what you think is a well-planned menu. You manage to get your work completed; you haven't noticed any severe changes in your appearance, but . . .

Do you get up in the morning full of vitality? If not, it's time to take inventory of your eating habits.

1. Are you a city dweller who eats like a farmer, thinking you should consume three large meals a day?
2. Are you one of those people who has only coffee for breakfast, a quick sandwich for lunch, and then crams a day's supply of calories into your evening meal?
3. Are you an "apple pie for breakfast" gal, who has to have dessert with every meal?
4. Do you pay more attention to taste than to nutrition?
5. Are you a snacker?

If you answer in the affirmative to any of these questions, it's time for a change.

You will be able to see an immediate difference in the shape of your figure by following these rules:

1. NEVER EAT LARGE AMOUNTS OF FOOD AT ANY ONE TIME. Five small meals a day provide you with the same nourishment as three large ones and eliminate that overstuffed feeling. Your body can assimilate only so much food at one time, and any unnecessary carbohydrates will be stored as fat.
2. DON'T GET BY ON STIMULANTS. Even though coffee and sugar products stimulate a feeling of energy, your body needs nutrients, particularly after a night's sleep.
3. NO DESSERT WITH YOUR MEALS. Desserts are surplus, but if you feel you must have one occasionally, the best time to eat it is between meals. You should select your dessert from fruits, cheesecake or egg custard, and the serving should be small.
4. SELECT YOUR FOOD FOR ITS NUTRITIONAL CONTENT. This will take time to learn, but it will have an effect on your children and your children's children. It would be wise to write to the Department of Agriculture for their book, *Composition of Foods, Raw, Processed and Prepared.* When ordering, ask for Agriculture

Handbook No. 8 which is sold by the Superintendent of Documents, U.S. Government Printing Office, Washington, D.C. 20402, at $1.50.

5. DON'T SNACK ON "DEAD" FOOD. I highly recommend snacking on foods high in nutrients, but those products put on the market for taste appeal only, are what I call "dead" foods. These are mostly starch and/or sugar and contribute nothing to your vitamin, mineral and protein requirements. A small snack before retiring is fine, but it should be food that is low in carbohydrates and calories. Follow the snack chart in this chapter.

These rules followed faithfully can completely change your figure proportions.

A friend of mine has been married for twelve years. After having two children, she can still give any teenager or co-ed competition on the beach in her bikini. She keeps her figure in perfect proportions by eating five small meals a day. Even though she sometimes eats small servings of dessert, she never eats them with her meals. Neither does she drink an entire cold drink at one time; it may last all day. If this routine can work for her, it can work for you!

Eating out does not give you license to overeat. Because you do not want to be wasteful, you may try to eat the entire portion. To avoid overeating, ask the waitress to put what is left in a bag for you to take home. A manager of one of the health salons I presided over taught me that lesson years ago. She maintains a 38-23-35 figure and has beautiful legs without the slightest bulge on her thighs. In all the years I worked with her, I never saw her eat a large meal.

You will have much more energy and be more alert by eating small quantities of food at a time. You'll never have that after-meal slump. The time you used to spend digesting the surplus can be put to creative use. I promise you, you will learn to love this form of eating. If you are a working girl, use your coffee break to have a few bites of something nutritional (after you get back from a brisk walk).

COMPLEXION—SKIN TONE

Have you ever wondered why some people show aging so much earlier than others? There are some factors beyond our control, such as heredity, but much can be done to maintain youthful skin. You should become aware of factors involved in bringing about premature aging of the skin, so you can take steps to delay this process. For example, aching feet make wrinkles.

Vitamins have a definite effect on your skin and complexion. B_2 and B_6 vitamins are beneficial to your nervous system, and thus are fundamental for well being, for your nervous system affects every part of your body. If you are lacking in the B vitamins, your breathing can be hampered, stress can be put on your heart and your circulatory system can be affected. You may have poor elimination due to nerves and impaired efficiency. All of these things trigger changes in your skin. One of the first signs of irregularity is blemishes. Poor circulation gives you a dry skin. Unfortunately, a deficiency of vitamins will often not show up for years. Just because you have no problem today, do not take this precious state for granted. It is a condition far easier to prevent than to cure.

In order to prevent premature wrinkles, your daily diet must contain sufficient amounts of tissue and muscle building proteins. Your complexion, as well as other parts of your body, can be kept youthful mostly by the protein foods which supply all the essential amino acids. If you are getting inadequate supplies of proteins, tissues begin to sag, causing wrinkles. Complexion proteins are found in meats, cheese, milk, eggs and legumes. Your diet must also be rich in vitamin C. Between the protein cells of the skin is a cementing substance, collagen, which needs a sufficient supply of vitamin C. Oranges, grapefruit and tomatoes are all rich in vitamin C.

Vitamins help keep your skin lovely from the inside, and here are a few tips on external aids:

1. Bathe with unscented cleansing cream instead of water, as soap and water are very drying. Apply the cream to a small portion of your body at a time and wipe off with terry toweling. Use soap and water on personal areas only.
2. When using body lotion, wet your skin before applying lotion. This will help retain the skin's moisture.
3. Have a humidifier in your home and use it both winter and summer. The degree of humidity will vary with the atmospheric conditions where you live. If there is much moisture in the air, you will not need to produce it synthetically.

A THOUGHT TO BE REMEMBERED: Everything you think and everything you do shows results in your face, whether the emotions are ugly or beautiful. Good thoughts are as important as vitamins.

MORE ENERGY

How many times have you said, "If I just had the energy . . ."? There is no magic formula, but regardless of your age, if you practice the suggestions in this chapter, you'll find your energy increasing. One of my first rules is never to rely on coffee, tea, pep pills or cold drinks for stimulants. These will only decrease your real energy potential. If you do not possess the energy for an activity and you take a false stimulant to perform the job, you are forcing your body to perform beyond its normal level. When your body is overworked without proper nourishment, it draws its need for nutrients from your body cells. This puts you in a run-down condition, making you susceptible to disease. Disease, in turn, weakens your body even more. When you are ill or recovering from an operation, you need more vitamins, minerals and protein to rebuild your strength. Wouldn't it be better to allow nature to assist and take the necessary time? Put more vitamins in your diet and in return, you'll receive more energy.

ARE YOU NERVOUS?

If your diet is insufficient in the B vitamins, you may develop a nervous condition. Nervousness often compels one to eat, using food as a pacifier. When your body is overfed, it is pacified right into a state of lethargy. You may think you are less nervous, but you are actually only apathetic, due to an overstuffed feeling. In this condition, you move slowly and therefore burn up fewer calories. This, of course, causes an increase in your weight. All for the lack of a little B vitamin.

GOOD VISION

My grandmother used to tell me to eat raw carrots so that I could see in the dark. For a long time, I thought it was just an "old wives' tale," but there was more truth in her admonition than I realized. The retina of the eye contains a pigment which is composed of vitamin A and protein. When the eye is exposed to light, some of the vitamin A is lost; the pigment is regenerated when a fresh supply of vitamin A is available. Night blindness results when this regeneration does not take place. Carrots do not actually contain vitamin A, since it is found only in foods of animal origin. What they do contain is a substance called carotene, which is converted into vitamin A in the body. For this reason, carotene is often called provitamin A.

BEAUTIFUL HAIR

Every woman wants beautiful hair, hair a man loves to run his fingers through. The following are excellent rules for shining, healthy hair:

1. Shampoo at least once a week with a nonalkaline shampoo.
2. Brush 100 strokes a day.
3. If hair is bleached, tinted or subjected to much sun, use a conditioner after each shampoo.
4. Avoid excessive sun and wind.

You must realize, however, that your hair cannot be healthier at the ends than at the roots. What comes out of these roots depends on two factors: the texture of your hair (which is inherited) and your state of health.

5. Circulation is one of the secrets to healthier hair. Exercise until your face is flushed. After all exercise periods, lie on a slant board with your feet at the elevated end and pull your hair until you feel a warm, tingling flow of blood in your scalp.
6. Never wear a tight hat.
7. Do not roll hair in tight curlers and leave for long periods at a time.
8. Do not wear a pony tail for long periods of time, as this may cause loss of hair.

The B vitamins play an important part in the health of your hair. If you have ever had a severe illness or an operation, you probably noticed a difference in your hair. It may have become dry and brittle. This, no doubt, was caused by an acute shortage of vitamins and minerals. You need more vitamins and minerals when illness occurs and if your body is not supplied with them, it draws them from your tissues and body cells, causing a deficiency. As with your skin, this shows up in the condition of your hair. Avoid hair that gives away your age by its color, texture and dullness by supplying your body with its needs before the aging process starts to take its toll.

Fifty million people in the United States go on reducing diets each year. Out of that fifty million, only one hundred thousand obtain results. Out of that, only fifty thousand maintain their goal. One reason might be that they go into it without preparation. If you are serious about this plan, have available all the ammunition needed to fight the battle of the bulge.

Remember, this is a war against a lifetime of bad eating habits. You have been feeding your mental computer the wrong source of information by selecting what you eat for these two reasons: 1. To fill your stomach, 2. For enjoyment, regardless of consequence.

Until you can analyze your food in the following manner, chances are you will return to your old habits:

1. In what form does this food come to me; how much processing has taken place and why?
2. How can I best prepare this food for the greatest nutritional value?
3. What am I getting out of my meals in the way of vitamins, minerals, protein, carbohydrates, fats?

It is suggested that you write the Dept. of Agriculture for their "Home And Garden" Bulletin #90. Nutrition-wise, you will find it of great help.

COOKING LOSSES

Cooking cereals in excessive quantities of water, draining off the cooking water and rinsing afterward waste nutrients.

Some persons persist in washing rice before cooking. This is an unnecessary step because today's packaged rice has already been cleaned. Moreover, washing is nutritionally expensive. Washing rice once before cooking can cause a thiamine loss of 25 percent in regular white rice, and a loss of 10 percent in brown or parboiled rice. This loss may be important in diets of persons who eat a great deal of rice.

You may have noticed these directions on some rice packages: "To retain vitamins, do not rinse before or drain after cooking."

The nutrients in rice are well-retained if rice is cooked in just enough water to be absorbed during the cooking period.

Cooking causes little loss of nutrients from ready-to-cook breakfast foods, such as rolled oats, rolled wheat, hominy grits, cracked wheat, farina and others. Many of the breakfast cereals on the market are precooked and require only minutes to prepare.

When baking keep the product in the oven only until the crust is light brown.

Limit the surface area exposed to heat. For example, less thiamine is lost when cornbread is baked as a loaf than when the same batter is baked in sticks.

Toasting causes additional loss of thiamine. However, the thicker the slice of bread and the lighter the finished product, the smaller is the loss of thiamine.

One comparison showed a toasting loss to be only half as great in a thick slice as a thin slice.

Riboflavin, another B vitamin in cereals, is not greatly affected by heat but is sensitive to light. Experimental studies of riboflavin loss in commercially baked bread indicate that heavy waxed paper or other translucent covering protects the riboflavin in bread very well.

BE VITAMIN-WISE WHEN YOU SELECT VEGETABLES

— In general, freshly harvested vegetables have more vitamins than those held in storage.

— Make full use of vine-ripened tomatoes in summer when they are plentiful and inexpensive. Tomatoes vine ripened out-of-doors in summer sunlight have twice as much vitamin C as tomatoes grown in greenhouses in winter.

— You get several times as much vitamin A value from bright-orange, mature carrots as from pale-colored, young ones. Even so, young carrots are a good source of vitamin A: choose them if you prefer.

— Choose deep-orange sweet potatoes for maximum vitamin A value.

— Among the vegetables, turnip greens, kale and collards are good sources of riboflavin as well as of vitamins A and C. Lima beans, peas, and young cowpeas, including black-eye peas, contribute appreciable amounts of thiamine and protein.

— Peppers are high in vitamins A and C.

— Leaf lettuce has more vitamin A value than pale-green head lettuce. The dark-green, outer leaves of head lettuce are much higher in vitamin A value than the inner leaves.

— Potatoes, although not rich in vitamin C, are a good source of this nutrient when eaten regularly.

— If the tops of beets are attached and still tender when you buy them, cook them—they are rich in vitamin A value.

The importance of vitamin C has been stressed, but I urge you to remember this: for radiant health and well being, you must have some vitamin C each day, whether in citrus fruits or vegetables. For the sources of vitamins and minerals in your diet, refer to the charts that follow.

Name of the nutrient	*Foods that supply important amounts*	*Some reasons why you need it*
	3 NUTRIENTS FOR SPECIAL JOBS + ENERGY	
Protein	Meat, fish, poultry, eggs All kinds of cheese Milk Cereals and breads Dried beans and peas Peanut butter, nuts	To build and repair all tissues in the body To help form substances in the blood which are called "antibodies" and which fight infection To supply energy
Fat	Butter and cream Salad oils and dressings Cooking fats Fat meats	To supply a large amount of energy in a small amount of food To help keep skin smooth and healthy by supplying substances called "essential fatty acids"
Carbohydrate (Sugars and Starches)	Breads and cereals Potatoes and corn Bananas Dried fruits, sweetened fruits Sugar, syrup, jelly, jam, honey	To supply energy To carry other nutrients present in the food
	VITAMINS	
Vitamin A	Yellow fruits, dark green and yellow vegetables Butter, whole milk, cream, Cheddar-type cheese, ice cream Liver	To help keep skin smooth and soft To keep nervous system healthy and resistant to infection To protect against night-blindness
Vitamin B_1 or Thiamine	All meats, fish and poultry—pork supplies about 3 times as much as other meats Eggs Enriched & whole grain breads, cereals Milk White potatoes	To keep appetite and digestion normal To keep nervous system healthy To help prevent irritability To help body release energy from food

Riboflavin	Milk All kinds of cheese Ice cream Meats, fish, poultry Eggs	To help cells use oxygen To help keep vision clear To help prevent cracking at the corners of the mouth To help keep skin and tongue smooth To help prevent scaly, greasy skin around mouth and nose
Vitamin C or Ascorbic Acid	Citrus fruits—lemon, orange grapefruit, lime Strawberries, cantaloupe Tomatoes Green peppers, broccoli Raw greens, cabbage White potatoes	To make cementing materials that hold body cells together To make walls of blood vessels firm To help resist infection To help prevent fatigue To help in healing wounds and broken bones
Vitamin D or The sunshine vitamin	Vitamin D milk Butter Fish liver oil Sunshine (not a food!)	To help the body absorb calcium from digestive tract To help build calcium and phosphorus into bones
	MINERALS	
Calcium	Milk Cheese, especially Cheddar-type Ice cream Turnip and mustard greens Collards and kale	To help build bones, teeth To help make blood clot To help muscles react normally To delay fatigue and help tired muscles recover
Iron	Liver Meat and eggs Green leafy vegetables Raisins, dried apricots	To combine with protein to make hemoglobin, the red substance in the blood that carries oxygen to the cells

RECOMMENDED DAILY DIETARY ALLOWANCES

Allowances are intended for persons normally active in a temperate climate

AGE	PROTEIN	CALCIUM	IRON	VIT A	THIAMINE	RIBOFLAVIN	NIACIN EQUIVALENT	ASCORBIC ACID	VIT D
	Grams	Grams	Mg.	I.U.*	Mg.	Mg.	Mg.	Mg.	I.U.*
				WOMEN					
18-35	58	0.8	15	5,000	0.8	1.3	14	70	—
35-55	58	.8	15	5,000	.8	1.2	13	70	—
55-75	58	.8	10	5,000	.8	1.2	13	70	—
				MEN					
18-35	70	.8	10	5,000	1.2	1.7	19	70	—
35-55	70	.8	10	5,000	1.0	1.6	17	70	—
55-75	70	.8	10	5,000	.9	1.3	15	70	—
				GIRLS					
12-15	62	1.3	15	5,000	1.0	1.5	17	80	400
15-18	58	1.3	15	5,000	.9	1.3	15	70	400

* International Unit

Another valuable publication put out by the Department of Agriculture is "Nutritive Value of Food," Home and Garden Bulletin No. 72. This is very similar to the "Composition of Foods" mentioned earlier in this chapter, but is more compact in its information and the price is only 25¢.

Using these suggestions, you will find every well planned nutritional meal a thrilling experience, knowing you are eating your way toward a more beautiful, healthier you. You will be rewarded daily.

Perhaps the hunger you have had all year has been for a younger, more curvaceous body, keener mind and better health. Feed that hunger with youth-giving food. Let this be the beginning for you. Mark this date down and next year at this time celebrate your birthday along with your new measurements.

First let's take inventory of the food stocked in your kitchen and replace the "dead foods" such as cookies, candy, cake, pastry, pretzels, potato chips or corn chips, white bread, crackers, and any other starchy "fillers." Replace them with foods which contain needed vitamins, minerals and protein.

Here are some of the items you should look for on your grocery shelves: Variety of vegetables, fresh fruits in season, plus lemons, apples and oranges, fresh green spinach to be used for salad, or leaf lettuce, dried skimmed milk, canned salmon, variety of meat (including hamburger), tomatoes, cottage cheese and regular cheese, broth, carrots (fresh), raisins. You may have to try the health food store for these: wheat germ, herb tea, dried brewer's yeast, yogurt, peanut butter (with natural oils).

Buy the items on this list as soon as possible to start your new way of life. I would also suggest you take a vitamin tablet for 30 days at least to help you overcome your past nutritional deficiencies. I feel it's better to take organic vitamins.

BREAK YOUR PRESENT EATING HABITS AND GIVE YOUR BODY A REST

If you are overweight, your body has been working overtime seven days a week, 365 days a year. It's only fair to give it a few days off a couple of times a year. You know how refreshed you feel from a weekend away from your work? You will have that same refreshing feeling when you give your inner body a chance to rest. Let it have three days without being abused with the intake of excessive hard-to-digest foods.

If you are not overweight, but your figure is out of proportion, it's a good idea to use this diet to break your habit of overeating at any one meal.

BREAKFAST	8:00 A.M.	1 large orange (sectioned) 1 cup hot herb tea with 1 teaspoon honey and 1 slice of lemon
SNACK	10:00	1 small glass vegetable juice
LUNCH	12:00	1 cup hot broth or raw vegetable salad or 3 large tablespoons cottage cheese with 1 slice pineapple (unsweetened)
SNACK	2:00 P.M.	1 small glass apple juice
SNACK	4:00	1 small glass apple juice
DINNER	6:00	1 cup hot broth or bouillon 1 garden fresh salad
SNACK	8:00	1 tablespoon cottage cheese or 1 cup hot water with 2 tablespoons dried skimmed milk

REDUCING DIET

BREAKFAST	8:00 A.M.	1 fresh orange 1 poached or boiled egg 1 slice broiled or baked ham 1 cup herb tea (no sugar)
SNACK	10:00	½ cup bouillon
LUNCH	12:00	1 small hamburger patty 2 slices tomato on lettuce leaf 1 glass fresh carrot juice or 1 of the salads listed in this chapter
SNACK	3:00 P.M.	½ cup bouillon
DINNER	6:00	3 oz. lean meat, fish, poultry or cottage cheese 1 raw vegetable 1 cooked vegetable (small serving)
SNACK	8:00	½ cup bouillon

FIGURE PROPORTIONING DIET

BREAKFAST	8:00 A.M.	½ grapefruit 1 egg 1 slice ham 1 glass fresh carrot juice or 1 glass skimmed milk

SNACK	10:00	1 inch square of cheese
LUNCH	12:00	1 slice 100% whole wheat bread
		1 heaping tablespoon peanut butter mixed with
		1 tablespoon honey
		1 glass skimmed milk
SNACK	3:00 P.M.	1 fruit of your choice (fresh)
DINNER	6:00	4 oz. lean meat, fish, poultry or cottage cheese
		1 raw vegetable
		1 cooked vegetable
		1 cup herb tea

WEIGHT GAINING DIET

BREAKFAST	8:00 A.M.	2 eggs
		2 slices whole wheat toast
		1 slice ham or 3 slices bacon
		2 pats butter
		1 tablespoon honey
SNACK	10:00	1 peanut butter and honey sandwich
LUNCH	12:00	1 cheese sandwich made with whole wheat bread
		1 glass milk
		½ cup dates
SNACK	3:00 P.M.	1 banana milkshake
DINNER	6:00	1 bowl cream soup (your choice)
		2 servings meat, fish, poultry or cottage cheese
		1 raw vegetable
		1 cooked vegetable
SNACK	8:00	1 peanut butter sandwich

If you are on the reducing or figure proportioning diet, it is not necessary to have the snacks suggested in the morning or midafternoon unless you are hungry before mealtime. You should never let yourself get extremely hungry as this could cause you to overeat at meal time. A snack also keeps your blood sugar from dropping. When your blood sugar drops, you begin to feel fatigue. You be the judge as to whether or not you need the snack.

SNACK SUGGESTIONS

For Reducing:

Raw celery, watercress, chicory, endive, cucumber, escarole, lettuce, parsley, radish, raw cauliflower, carrots and bouillon

Figure Proportioning:

Fresh fruit of any kind, 1 teaspoon peanut butter, ¼ cup cottage cheese with lettuce, 1 oz. slice of cheese with lettuce, 1 glass skimmed milk, 1 small glass vegetable juice, 1 large tablespoon salmon or tuna without oil

Gaining Weight:

Tuna fish in oil, avocados, dried raisins, apricots, prunes, peaches, dates, apples, peanuts (raw preferred)

Beverage:

For better health avoid stimulant beverages. Suggestion for beverage: fresh fruit juice, tomato juice, herb teas; refreshing glass of water is also a good choice

SOME OF MY FAVORITE SALADS

1 cup fresh spinach (break leaves in pieces)
½ boiled egg (boiled slowly to retain more protein)
1 heaping tablespoon grated cheese
1 slice boiled ham, cut into slices ¼ inch wide
½ large carrot (large slices)
¼ tomato diced as desired
    sprinkle top with
2 tablespoons wheat germ

Large lettuce leaves
¼ can pink salmon (drained)
½ carrot sliced in strips
    top with
1 sliced fresh hard boiled egg

---

2 lettuce leaves
5 large tablespoons cottage cheese
1 round slice unsweetened pineapple
    top with
1 cherry

---

2 dark-green lettuce leaves
1 whole unpeeled apple, grated
3 heaping tablespoons grated cheese
1 tablespoon raisins

If you carry your lunch you could mix this and put it in a Thermos bottle, or you could drink ½ at your morning coffee break, ½ in the afternoon, unless you are on a strict reducting diet. If so wait until you have proper figure proportions. Mix all of the following in your blender with two or three cubes of ice.

Refreshing lunch with apricot influence:

3 dried apricots
½ cup powdered skim milk
1 teaspoon honey
¾ cup cold water

Refreshing lunch with prune influence:

3 dried prunes
½ cup powdered skim milk
1 teaspoon honey
¾ cup cold water

Quick pick-up drink:

1 glass orange juice
1 egg
1 tablespoon wheat germ
1 teaspoon honey

Banana shake:

½ cup dried skim milk
½ cup water
1 ripe banana
1 teaspoon blackstrap molasses or honey

Fruit punch:

½ cup orange juice, unsweetened
1 slice unsweetened pineapple
½ ripe banana
2 cherries
1 tablespoon honey

MIDMORNING AND MIDAFTERNOON PICK-UP FOR THE WOMAN SERIOUSLY OVERWEIGHT

1 small glass carrot juice or

1 glass tomato juice or

1 glass orange juice or

1 glass grapefruit juice or

1 glass mixed vegetable juice

More delicious nutritious drinks to mix in your blender:

1 pint skimmed milk
½ cup dried skim milk
3 dried peaches
1 tablespoon raisins
1 teaspoon honey

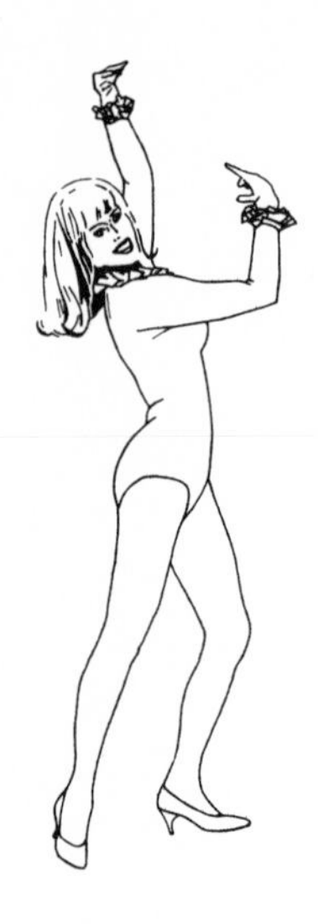

BECOME A TANTALIZING FEMALE

Ninety percent of the women in America, and many in other lands, are irritable and tense. They are often so taut they appear ready to snap like a fiddle string. Pressures mount and their blood pressure gets higher and higher. It shows in their dry skin, lifeless hair and brittle nails. It shows in their posture, their appearance and their expressions. And what is showing is ugly. Tension and frustration are the worst enemies beauty can have.

Read a book or a poem where a man is describing a beautiful, sexy woman. Does he picture her going in fifty directions at once? Does he picture her tense, upset or frustrated? Does he picture her stiff, self-conscious or awkward? Never. The dream woman to whom men pay homage is quiet, composed, poised. Please note that these are not the same as lazy or sloppy. It is a self-controlled woman as compared to a hectic disorganized one. The key words are graceful, poised, self-assured and coordinated. A desirable woman has a rhythmic body—every move she makes is a dance. Her dance may be beautiful and serene as a ballet, sleek and sexy as a panther or as uninhibited as a go-go dancer. No matter what it is—it is done rhythmically. A beautiful woman can never be awkward. Her arms and her entire body should move easily in coordination with each part of her. This is a tantalizing woman.

"That may be fine," I can hear you saying, "but where do I come in? I can't dance." Mistake number one. All children are born with an inherent sense of rhythm. But the inhibitions and disciplines of adult society tend to deaden that natural sense. If you have done little dancing since you were a child, it is no wonder that you aren't competing with Juliet Prowse right now. She has developed her ability while you let yours grow stale. Even though you ignored your ability, you probably have a secret desire to dance. You watch those who can dance with fascination and envy. When you are alone in the house and you hear music on the radio or record player, you probably move in a timid dance of your own. Maybe you just sway back and forth. It is a woman's heritage to love beautiful things. This must assuredly include beautiful music—to which you love to see beautiful movements. Music creeps under your skin and begs to be expressed in motion, motion which will add to the beauty of the music and express the beauty within your soul. As a woman, with beauty in your heart and soul, you owe it to yourself to learn to express it with your body. A perfect figure will make you pretty or attractive, but a body that can move with grace becomes beauty incarnate.

When you see a dance performed, you see thousands of separate movements put together for the final effect. No wonder you find it hard to follow a dance you see being performed. That dancer spent weeks perfecting each small gesture, so don't be discouraged if you can't do it in three minutes. In the following chapters, we will break down the motions into their separate parts so that you may master them individually. Then you will be able to combine them into the dances we will give you, and finally into your own creations. Don't, however, start to think of these as mere dance steps. Each movement was chosen not only to help you move more gracefully, but also to exercise your body into a more beautiful figure.

Each section of your body must function differently and must be trained in the way it is to function. You trained your body to walk, now you can train it to be rhythmic and coordinated. The shoulder roll is a good example, it is used in thousands of dances. Besides being useful in dancing, it will also give you a health workout. It helps release tension in the back muscles, and in the neck—helping avoid a dowager's hump. It also helps the blood circulation. All this while it's making you a more tantalizing, vibrant woman.

Then there is the rib cage. When isolated, movements of the rib cage are Oriental. Yet, the rib cage or torso is the base for almost every movement of which your body is capable. To train the rib cage to move correctly, is to give a good basis on which to build your feminine image.

Next, there are the hips, thighs and abdomen. Your good health depends very much upon keeping them trim and firm. Your figure and sex appeal also depend on this. Through dancing, it is possible to get them that way. Here, however, is a good example of where you must select what dances you do or your figure will suffer. A ballet dancer inevitably has overdeveloped thighs. For her art, it is essential to develop them that much, and I'm sure she feels her dancing is well worth the sacrifice of trim thighs. You, however, probably have no intention of devoting your life to ballet. Your aims are to learn some ballet for the grace it can teach you, while avoiding those exercises which would overdevelop your thighs. That is why we have carefully screened the movements we will give you, so that you may be assured that following this book will truly enhance your body—not just teach you dancing. As far as the hips are concerned, their motions in dancing are sexually oriented, and the woman desiring sex appeal must master these immediately. Since the hips are also used in such mundane chores as walking, no one cannot afford to skip these dance movements. The motions of the hips while dancing will give you a much better, more coordinated stride.

These movements, plus those of the arms, legs, hands, feet, neck and face, are the parts that will culminate in a final dance. When you put on a record and fuse the shoulder roll, arm movements, hips, torso and legs into a thousand and one dances, then you will give praises that you took time to recapture your gift of rhythm. You will marvel at this wonderful talent which was buried inside you and left for dead. Through awakening it, you will awaken to a more beautiful, more creative, more healthy and more feminine life.

Now you are embarking on an exciting new adventure to an exciting new you. Forget everything else. Forget the grocery bill, the problem with the dishwasher, Johnny's low math grades, Suzie's attachment for an unsuitable friend . . . Think only of this: God has created you as a UNIQUE human being. You are a bundle of genes unlike any other arrangement of genes in this world. Throw off the shackles of routine existence which are paralyzing the positive, creative emotions deep inside you. Start the music. Dance! Stretch! Allow these movements to become hymns of gratitude for being you—let them become paeans of joy. Release that within you that you have always thought beyond your reach.

Listen to the music. Let it penetrate the pores of your body. Listen with a third ear which is deep within you. Bend . . . twist . . . step . . . skip . . . run . . . lose yourself. Forget yourself.

You and the music are one. The music is you. And you are the most beautiful music ever created. For the moment, step out of your skin and merge with that powerful unrestrainable, irresistible force within you. Come . . . Dancercize with me to a brand-new, TANTALIZING you.

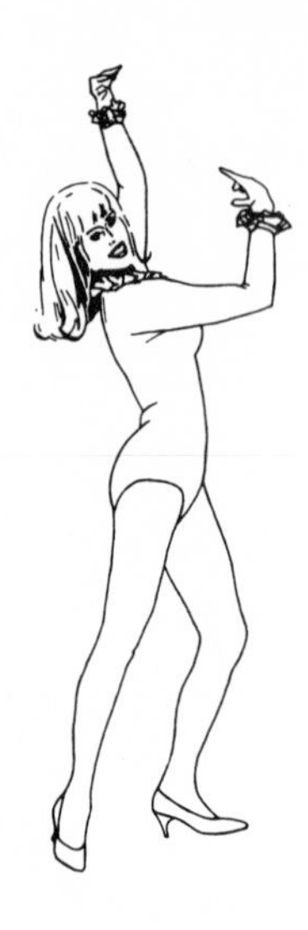

SIX WEEKS TO A MORE BEAUTIFUL YOU

Now you are ready to get down to the action you have been looking forward to, but before you start the "Dancercize," it is important for you to know how to breathe correctly.

1. With teeth together and lips open, make a *ssssss* sound until you are out of breath.
2. Now close your lips and feel your rib cage expand as air rushes in. Put your hands on each side of your rib cage. Repeat the above exercise five times. When you inhale, your hands should be closer together; as your lungs fill with air, your hands spread apart. This will help you to know if you are breathing correctly with the lower chest, rather than with the upper chest.

Practice this method of breathing with all the "dancercizes," inhaling on the starting position and exhaling as you leave the second position.

Do each "dancercize" only the number of times called for in the explanation, and practice in front of a full-length mirror, if possible. Music is a must and you should have some good 4/4 music on when you do any of the "dancercizes."

FIRST WEEK

Read the introductions to:

Face Your Future

Shoulders, Arms and Back
Beauty and Your Bustline
Heavenly Hands
Waistline—Lifeline
Perfecting the Pelvis
The Fashionable Derriere
The Leggier Look

Do Basic "dancercize" of each section *ONLY.*

SECOND WEEK

Do Beginning "dancercizes" only.

THIRD WEEK

Do Intermediate "dancercizes" only.

FOURTH WEEK

Do Advanced "dancercizes" only.

FIFTH WEEK

Do Combination for coordination only.

SIXTH WEEK

Select your favorites from any section.

FACE YOUR FUTURE

The chin and neckline are areas where many women first reveal their age. Nothing tells your age like a double chin and a loose throat. Many women would rather die than tell their age, but a double chin is all of the telltale evidence you need, because a double chin is impossible to conceal.

Most double chins come from overweight and faulty posture. Diet and Dancercize will take care of the first. Holding your head up high and keeping your shoulders down will help correct the second.

Just doing an exercise for reducing a double chin is not enough attention given to that area. As any model or movie star will tell you, a big part of a woman's charm lies in the small tilt of a head. The control, ease and sureness in which she handles her movements can convey a message without speaking one word. With the tilt of the head you can become flirty, draw your head in and you become shy, hold your head regal and you become a queen. Every thought can be conveyed in the way you use your head.

The following chin and neckline dancercizes will not only reduce the double chin, but as an added bonus will give you the control you need to relay your feminine charms without saying a word.

Head up girls, and FACE YOUR FUTURE.

THE SWAN (Basic)
Starting position 1. In a reverent mood, place your hands crossed at your neck.
2. Stand regal like a swan, pulling in your stomach and tightening your buttocks muscles.

3. Sustaining your movement, pull your shoulders down with pressure in your body and bend your head back as far as you can. Do five times, do not increase.

THE FLIRT (Basic)
Starting position 1. With your shoulders down and your arms at your side and facing straight ahead.
2. Tilt your head to the right until you feel a pull in your neck muscles, raise the shoulder to meet the head.
3. Return to starting position and repeat to the other side. Do five times to start with, and work up to ten daily.

SASSY SHOULDER PULL (Beginning)
Starting position 1. Place your right hand firmly behind your back and your left hand on your left shoulder. Be sure to keep your head erect and your shoulders down.
2. Tilt your head as far to the right as possible, pulling your left shoulder down.
3. Return to starting position.
4. Change your arms and repeat to the left. Do five times to start, and work up to ten times.

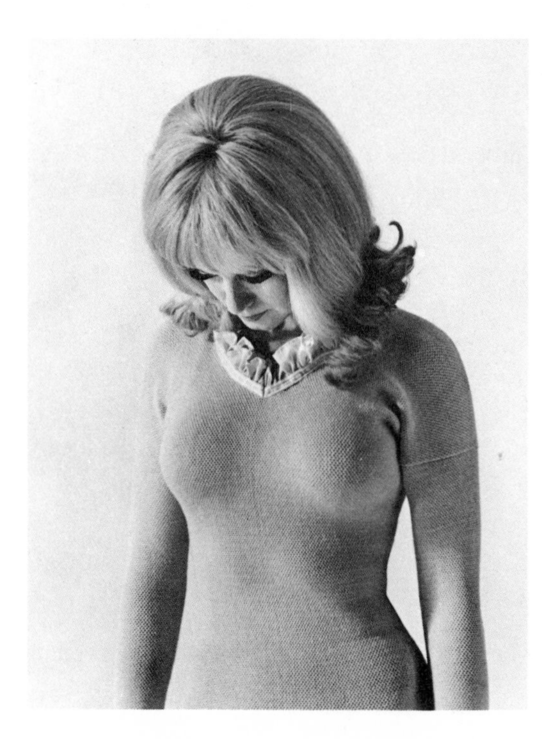

SEDUCTIVE PUPPET
(Beginning)

Starting position 1. Keeping your shoulders pulled down, place your hand on the crown of your head.
2. Pull up as straight as you can, like a puppet on a string.
3. After you have the correct feeling of a straight back and sculptural posture, repeat the Dancerize with your hands down at your sides.
4. With your hands down at your sides, keep your body rigid and bend your head forward as far as possible.
5. You will find this Dancerize a particularly good tension reliever. Do five to start with, and work up to ten daily.

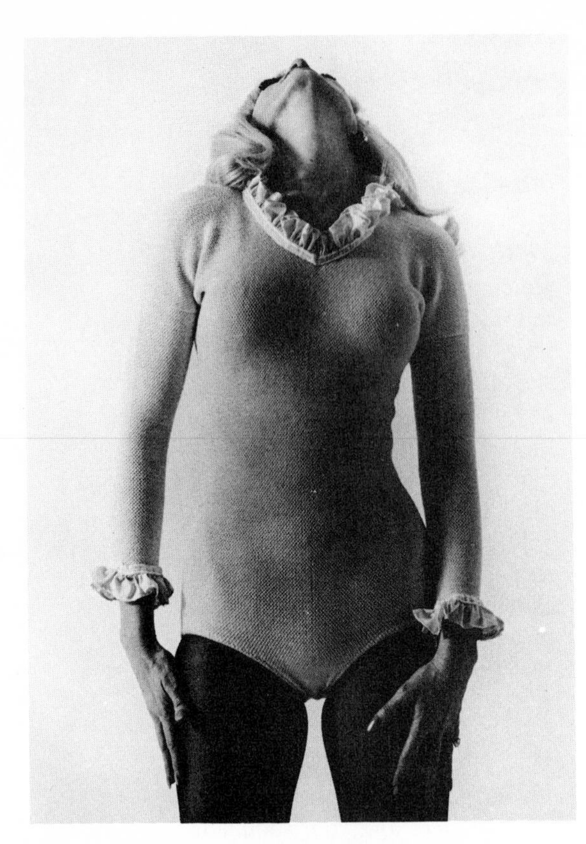

TANTALIZING TILT (Beginning)
Starting position 1. Place your arms down at your sides, face straight ahead, keeping your shoulders down.
2. Tilt your head to the right until you feel a pull in your neck.
3. Return to starting position, and repeat the tilt of your head to the left.
4. With shoulders remaining down, tilt your head back as far as possible.
5. Return to starting position. Do this five times to start, and work up to ten times.

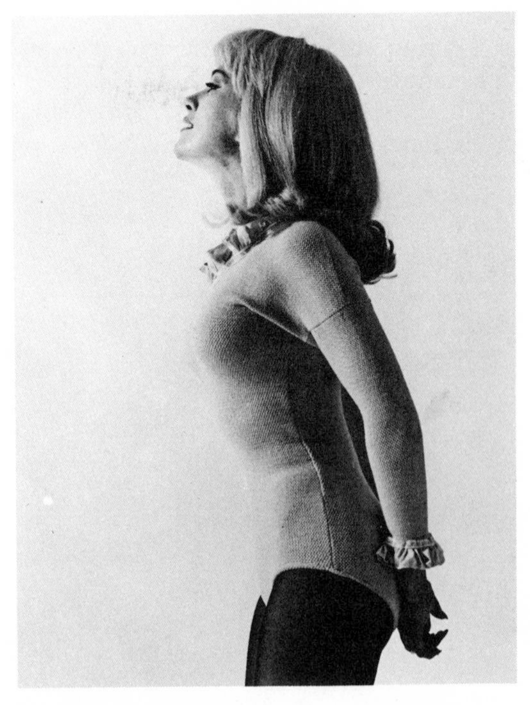

ORIENTAL NECK (Intermediate)
Starting position 1. Stand, holding the head high, shoulders down.
2. Place hands behind your back.
3. Extend your neck forward and at the same time pull your shoulders back, keeping your shoulders down.

SHY—BUT OH MY (Intermediate)
Starting position 1. With your arms comfortably at your sides and your head erect, extend your chin, reaching to the right side touching your collarbone.
2. Return to starting position.
3. Extend and reach with your chin touching your body as far down as possible.
4. Return to starting position.
5. Repeat to the left.
6. *Don't raise the shoulders to meet the head.* Let the head and the neck do the work. It is the pull on the neck and face muscles we are after. Do five to start, and work up to ten daily.

ANXIOUS ACCORDION (Intermediate)
Starting position 1. With your hands on your waist, pull your shoulders back with intensity.
2. Stretch your head forward.
3. Reverse the movement by stretching your head back.
4. Bring your elbows front.
Do five times to start, work up to ten times.

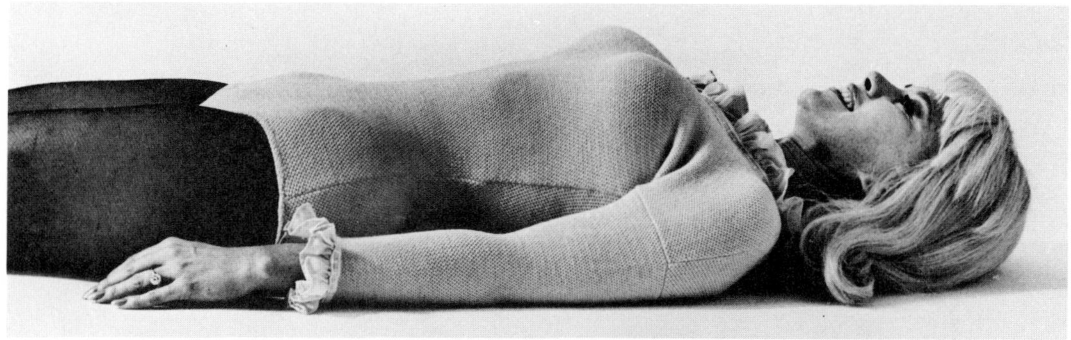

HAUGHTY HEAD LIFT (Advanced)
Starting position 1. Lie flat on the floor with your arms down at sides and palms down.
2. Thrust head back until your crown is resting on the floor.
3. Gracefully return to starting position.
Do five times to start, work up to ten times.

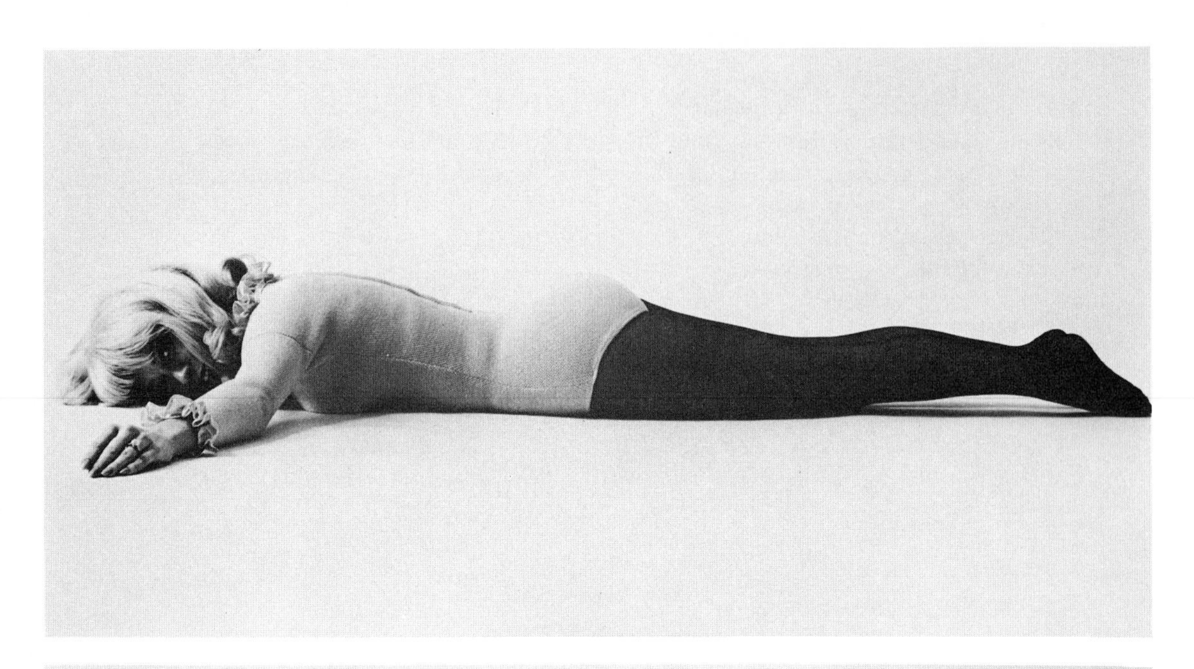

THE BIG PULL (Advanced)

Starting position 1. Lie flat on stomach, arms out at sides.

2. Raise head, arms, shoulders and chest as far off floor as possible.

3. Hold for count of four.

4. Pretend someone is pulling your head forward and your feet back. Relax. Start with four and increase daily.

ADVANCED HAUGHTY HEAD LIFT
Starting position 1. Lie flat on the floor, arms out at your sides.
2. Pull up and forward with your chest until your chest and head are off of the floor.
3. Return to starting position. Do five times to start, work up to ten times.

SHOULDERS – ARMS – BACK

I have been working with woman of all sizes, shapes and ages since 1954, and in all of this time I have known very few women to recognize the need for good posture and firm arms and back. Only the very heavy recognize this problem. One reason for this is that many women only have a front point of view, never turning their backs to the mirror. Don't you be one of those gals. Put down this book and go take a good look from the back.

Now that we are back together again, what did you see? Firm and youthful skin; not fat but a bit flabby; or public enemy number one—both fat and flabby?

As long as I have you depressed we might as well face a little more reality. Hold your left arm out to the side and pat the underneath area of your left arm with your right hand. Regardless of how slim you are, chances are that this area will need a little firming.

This chapter is doubly important because not only does every woman want to have firm and youthful back and shoulders, but she also wants to look and feel at ease in any situation at all times.

In order to have good posture, poise and command at all times you must have shoulder control. Raised shoulders relay tension or ill-at-easeness; shoulders too far forward give the impression of lack of confidence or fear of the situation; rounded back and shoulders tells the world you are sloppy or tired and gives you the "I don't care look." A little extra tip I learned that is worth practicing is when you are cold, don't tense your shoulders. It gives you an awkward appearance and will also make you colder. Next time, try to relax and see how much better you look and feel.

The following dancercizes will firm your back and arms, and relieve tension and improve your posture. Once you are able to do these in one continuous graceful, seductive movement, you'll find yourself coming alive as an exciting, tantalizing female.

HI HANDSOME (Basic)
Starting position 1. Place hands comfortably at sides, stand erect.
2. Roll both shoulders forward.
3. Roll shoulders up towards ceiling.
4. Roll shoulders back. Return to starting position.
Now that you have done all four positions, make the roll continuous, very smooth without stopping.

ARM CIRCLES (Beginning)
Starting position 1. Stand tall with arms out at sides.
2. Make a little circle with your arms.
3. Eight times forward.
4. Eight times backwards.

Be sure to keep your shoulders down and circle with intensity.
The following Dancercizes will help firm the *shoulders, back,* and *arms.* Be sure to keep your stomach in and buttocks muscles tucked under. *You must have tension in your body in order to derive the full benefits.* Tension in movement should be regarded as an increase of power.

YO-YO (Beginning)
Starting position 1. Stand erect with both arms at sides.
2. Raise your right shoulder up and pull down on your left shoulder.
3. Now reverse shoulders.
Start with eight, and increase daily.

HI THERE (Beginning)
Starting position 1. Lie flat on stomach, with head on floor.
2. Arms straight in front of head on floor.
3. Keep hips on floor and raise head, chest, and waist off of floor.
4. Hold for count of four, relax.
Do this ten times, and work up to thirty within fifteen days.

PEEK-A-BOO (Beginning)

Starting position 1. Sit on floor and draw legs up to chest.

2. Clasp hands around legs.

3. Bend head to knees, and round back.

4. Raising head up and a little back, straighten back.

Do this ten times, and work up to thirty within fifteen days.

TIGHTROPE (Beginning)
Starting position 1. Arms out to sides, stand erect.
2. Round shoulders forward as far as possible. Keep arms slightly rounded.
3. Keeping arms slightly rounded, pull shoulders back as far as possible.

FLIRTY (Beginning)
Starting position 1. Start with hands on front of thighs, round shoulders.
2. Pull shoulders back trying to touch shoulder blades. Place hands on buttocks muscles.

THE PUSH (Intermediate)
Starting position 1. With feet apart place weight on right leg.
2. Lean a little to the right, with right hand on right hip and left arm down straight at side.
3. Keeping shoulders down and elbow straight, raise left arm up to ceiling. Look to left hand.
4. Bending left elbow start bringing left arm down with tension.
5. Push arm down to starting position. Four times left arm, reverse weight and four times right arm.
Do this ten times to start, and work up to thirty times within fifteen days.

GRACE (Intermediate)
Starting position 1. For composure, delicacy and posture, start with arms rounded down in front.
2. Raise arms slowly out to sides, keeping palms down. Return to starting position (slowly).
Do this ten times, and work up to thirty within fifteen days.

THE BUTTERFLY (Intermediate)
Starting position 1. Keeping shoulders down start with both arms above head (palms turned out).
2. Push arms down with tension, bring right arm and shoulder front, left arm back. Return to starting position. Repeat to left.
Do ten times, and work up to thirty.

THE WESTERN PULL
(Intermediate)
Starting position 1. Sit on floor.
2. Bend knees with bottoms of feet together.
3. Keeping back straight, make a fist with your hands and place arms straight in front.
4. Bend elbow joints and pull arms back as far as possible.
Do this ten times, and work up to thirty within fifteen days.

FRAGILE (Intermediate)
Starting position 1. Stand upright, arms out at sides with palms down.
2. Slowly begin to raise your arms, turning your palms up.
3. Continue to raise your arms slowly to form a circle over your head. Be sure to keep your shoulders down.
4. Keeping arms above head lean to the right side. Return to starting position and repeat, leaning to left. Do this ten times, and work up to thirty within fifteen days.

COME UP AND SEE ME SOMETIME (Intermediate)
You will need to stand in front of the mirror until you have mastered this one.
Starting position 1. Stand erect with arms out to sides and pronated (palms turned down).
2. Keeping left shoulder still.
3. Move right shoulder with control, forward from shoulder socket.
4. Return to starting position.
5. Repeat to left. Do this ten times, and work up to thirty within fifteen days.

ARM PUSH (Advanced)
Starting position 1. Incline a little to the left. Raise both arms above your head.
2. Bend elbows and begin to push arms down.
3. Push arms the rest of the way down, straightening elbows.
Incline to the right and repeat Dancercize to left. (You must feel power and force in your arms. Pretend you are pushing water away.)
Do this ten times, and work up to thirty within fifteen days.

THE PENDULUM (Advanced)
Starting position 1. Standing tall place hands in front, resting lightly on thighs.
2. Swing arms to the right with stamina. Return to starting position, repeat to left.
Do this ten times, and work up to thirty within fifteen days.

DUET (Advanced)
Starting position 1. Stand erect in front of mirror.
2. Arms extended to sides, rounded slightly at the elbows. (Palms up)
3. Lean to the right from the waist keeping right palm in (palm up position). Turn your left palm down and keep arms rounded.
4. Repeat to left.
Repeat nine times more with smoothness and coordination and suppleness of these joints.

WIND IT UP (Advanced)
Starting position 1. Arms down at sides.
2. Make a big circle with your left arm, keeping your elbow joint straight. Bring your arm up in front.
3. Continue circling arm over head.
4. Continue circle, bring arm back.
Circle left arm eight times.
Circle right arm eight times.
Do this ten times to start, and work up to thirty within fifteen days.

THE COMPASS

(Advanced)

Starting position 1. Weight supported on both feet, with right arm out to side, left arm down at side.

2. Begin to make a compass (circle) with left arm slowly backwards.

3. Continue the compass, circling your left arm behind the back of your head.

4. Push left arm to right, level with right arm. Repeat to other side.

Do this ten times to start, and work up to thirty within fifteen days.

BEAUTY AND THE BUSTLINE

What woman does not want to have and maintain a good bustline to complete her picture? After all, a lovely bustline is the trademark of a perfect feminine figure. Increasing the bustline calls for patience. The exercises do not bring immediate results. They must be repeated regularly for a period of several months before an increase occurs. It will encourage you to know however, that you will increase circulation of blood in the pectoral muscles under the breast immediately.

It is important to pause after each ten counts of any bust exercise in which weights are used.

This is one area that almost every woman would like to have a miracle performed, because generally her bust is out of proportion with her hips. In order to balance the two areas we need weight. The reason your hips and thighs are so much heavier than the upper part of your body could be because your thighs and the trunk (hips) carry the body load. If you are carrying around extra weight it can even cause you to overdevelop in that area. Heavy weights used in any form strengthen and develop an area.

BEAUTY HINTS

1. To give the bust the appearance of being larger, buy a cotton stitched bra and do not iron after laundering.
2. If you have a heavy bust, change bra strap style so that you don't acquire indentation in your shoulders.
3. It is better to wear a bra a little bit big than too small. It makes you look larger and allows more air to pass through your clothing, especially a padded bra. Years ago women's busts would be wrapped tightly to make them appear smaller, but it actually made them smaller. The principle is not to girdle down your bust.
4. During pregnancy never go without a bra day or night and especially never go without one after the baby, and while you are nursing. Your bust may look and feel firm but once it is down to its normal size if you have gone without a bra you might find it sagging.
5. Nylon bras are very sexy, but unless padded they make you look smaller than stitched cotton.
6. Good posture can do a lot for the appearance of your bustline. Try this in front of a mirror: Keep your arms relaxed and down at your sides. Tuck your hips under, pull your tummy in and lift your chest without moving your arms.

The pectoral muscles which lie under the top part of the bust are rarely ever used, causing the chest to be underdeveloped.

Everyone responds to the bust exercises differently. Whether or not you gain in the tissue itself is an individual thing. Some women seem to gain in the bust from the stimulation of increased blood circulation in that area. Here is the system I have found to be most beneficial.

1. Start with 3 to 5 pound weights in each hand.
   Here is a list of suggestions to use as weights:
   a. One iron in each hand.
   b. Fill a number 2 or 3 can with cement.
   c. Two large books.
2. Do each exercise ten times every day for two weeks. Rest two weeks. After two weeks increase your repetitions to twenty of each exercise, resting after every ten. Rest two weeks and then do each exercise thirty times resting after each set of ten. Rest two weeks and then increase the weight in each hand 2 to 3 pounds and drop back down to doing each exercise ten times. Repeat the cycle adding weight after thirty repetitions of each exercise has been reached. The other method used in my book, *Debbie Drake's Easy Way to A Perfect Figure and Glowing Health,* is also excellent. It is just a matter of preference.
3. Lubricate the bust with oil before working out.
4. Do warm-up bust exercises before using weights.

FINGER PRESS (Basic and Warm-Up)
Starting position 1. Bend the elbows at chest level.
2. With the palms outstretched, let the fingers of one hand touch those of the other.
3. PRESS the fingers together as hard as you can. You will feel the pull as you press. Repeat twenty times or more.
This is an easy exercise that can be done from a seated or standing position. It firms and lifts the bust and tightens the upper arm. It is good for you whether you are trying to increase or decrease.
For best results do this exercise in the following manner:
Push, hold, count slowly 1, 2, 3.
Relax 1, 2, 3, breath deeply.
Repeat ten times daily, work up to twenty times daily.

WRIST PUSH (Basic and Warm-Up)
Starting position 1. Seated or standing position. Bend the elbows at chest level. Hold the left wrist with the right hand, the right wrist with the left hand.
2. PUSH the hands vigorously toward the elbows. Here again you will feel the action on the bust muscles as you push.
Repeat ten times daily, work up to twenty times daily.

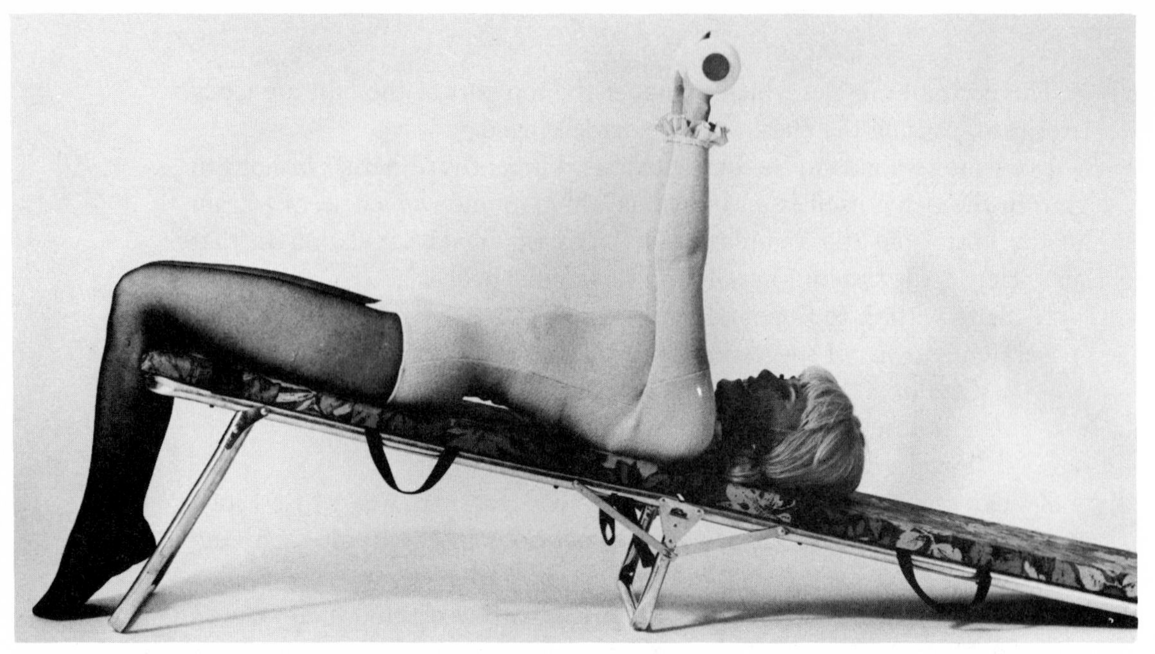

SINGLE PULLOVER (Beginning)
Starting position 1. Lie down on your back using either a slant board or some thing that will raise your legs and bottom portion of your body higher than your head.
2. Hold a book or bell weights in each hand. Keeping arms very straight, raise the weights up to the ceiling.
3. Extend left arm straight out towards left knee. Extend right arm (at the same time) back over the head, reaching as far back as possible. Return to starting position. The arms must be kept straight at all times.
Repeat ten times, alternating arms. Work up to thirty times.

ELBOW PUSH (Beginning)
Starting position 1. Be seated. Sit with legs crossed in front of you.
2. Hold a pillow between elbows.
3. PUSH the elbows together and release. PUSH with stamina so that you feel the power of the bust muscles as you push.
Repeat ten times, and work up to thirty times daily.

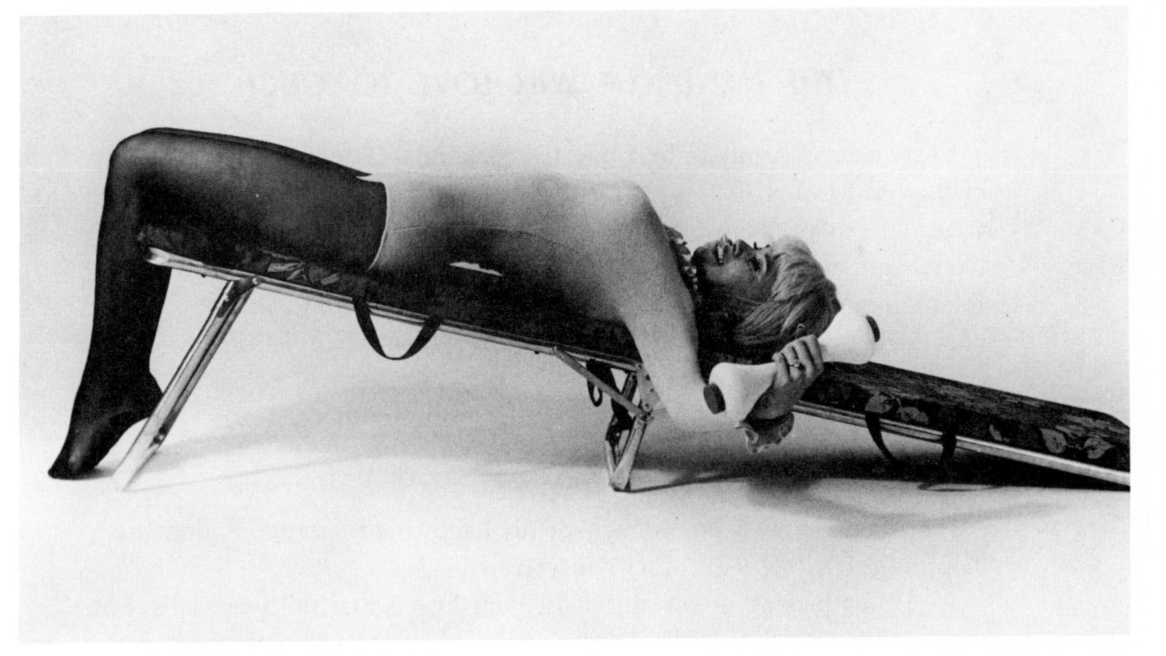

THE BARREL (Intermediate)
Starting position 1. Lie down on back on your slant board. Raise the arms above the chest as though you were holding a barrel.
2. Open the curved arms as widely as possible, pulling them way back.
3. Return arms to front of chest.
Repeat ten times, working up to thirty times daily.

DOUBLE PULLOVERS (Intermediate)
Starting position 1. Lie down on your back on slant board. Hold your weights in both hands.
2. Extend arms straight out toward knees.
3. Raise the weights over the head, reaching as far back as possible until they almost touch the floor, behind the head.
4. Return to starting position. Keeping arms straight at all times, repeat ten times. Work up to thirty times daily.

THE BIRD (Advanced)
Starting position 1. Lie down on your back on your slant board.
2. Keeping arms straight, raise arms and weights up to ceiling.
3. Bring weights down to chest, pulling elbows back as far as possible.
(Your elbows are the bird's wings.)
Repeat ten times, working up to thirty times daily.

THE CIRCLE FLIES (Advanced)
Starting position 1. Lie down on your back on a slant board. Extend arms to full length downward, hands touching.
2. Keeping elbows straight, raise the hands up to the sides of the head, as though you were drawing an arc.
3. When weights get up to head, turn the hands back to back.
Return to starting position bringing your arms downward in same cycle.
Repeat 10 times, working up to thirty times daily.

THE HANDS HE WILL LOVE TO TOUCH

Every woman wants to look and feel graceful and feminine from the tip of her head to her toes, and your hands and wrists are as much a part of your figure as your other proportions. Graceful, well-shaped hands will enhance your femininity while ugly awkward hands will distract from the total feminine picture. Hand dancercizes can be fitted into almost any part of your busy daily schedule. Many can be done while waiting in a car, talking on the telephone, watching television or other odd moments during the day when the hands are free.

HANDS

Dancercize alone is not enough—daily hand care is a must. Follow these helpful hints along with other dancercizes

1. When picking up an object use your fingers and not your nails. Put bobby pins on a table and pretend you have on wet nail polish, practice picking them up. Now do the same thing opening a drawer and taking something out of a drawer. This helps teach you how not to use your nails.
2. Every time you dry your hands push the cuticles back with your towel.
3. Before retiring put oil on your cuticles, lotion on your hands and wear soft gloves. This will help to make your hands feel silky and smooth.
4. A weekly manicure is a must even if you don't use polish.
5. Use rubber gloves anytime you have to put your hands in water and to do your housework.
6. A woman is never allowed to have dirty nails.
7. If your hands are one of your assets, you may use colored nailpolish and interesting rings to draw attention.
8. Never use nails to dial the telephone. Always use the end of a pen or some other object.
9. Many women use their hands excessively in conversation. It is all right if:
   a) The movements are feminine and graceful with the wrist and fingers relaxed.
   b) Nails are well manicured.
10. If you don't want to draw attention to your hands you should:
   a. Underplay them.

b. Avoid bright polish.
c. Avoid loud jewelry on fingers and wrists.

11. Gold jewelry and diamonds are more flattering than silver.
12. When you are driving or out in the sun or wind, wear gloves to protect your hands.

THE FIST (Basic)
Starting position 1. Standing upright make a fist and bend your arms to your chest.
2. Open your hands, spreading your fingers as far as possible.

COUNT DOWN (Beginning)
Starting position 1. Bend elbows, turn palms inward with fingers straight together.
2. Begin by bending your little fingers down.
3. Continue slowly one finger at a time.
4. Until all fingers are counted down.
Return to starting position.

INDIAN CHIEF
(Intermediate)
Starting position 1. For coordination of arms, stand erect.
2. Cross arms in front of you, elbows up.
3. Bending palms of hands back, raise left arm up.
Return to starting position and repeat to other side. Do ten times and work up to thirty within fifteen days.

HULA HANDS (Intermediate)

Starting position 1. Stand erect, arms out front with palms down.

2. Relax fingers.

3. Keeping arms still, turn palms in.

4. Continue the flow, turn your palms up toward the ceiling.

5. Turn palms facing each other, wrists together. Return to starting position and continue.

HINDU HANDS (Advanced)
Starting position 1. Standing tall, place elbows out and hands at chest.
2. Place thumb, index and second finger together and spread other two fingers as far apart as possible.
3. Keeping left arm in place extend right arm to side spreading fingers as far apart as possible.
4. Turn palm toward ceiling bringing little finger back toward wrist.
Return to starting position, and repeat to left.
5. Repeat four times each side and then extend both arms at the same time eight times.

LITTLE EGYPT (Advanced)
Starting position 1. Shoulders down, elbows bent and hands above head. Hands turned back to back (palms out).
2. Turn palms of hands in, palms touching and fingers pulled back.
3. Same position as above, place fingers touching.
4. Keeping hands together, bend hands back.
5. Keeping elbows out, bring hands down. Turn palms towards head with fingertips touching neck.
Do ten times, and work up to thirty within fifteen days.

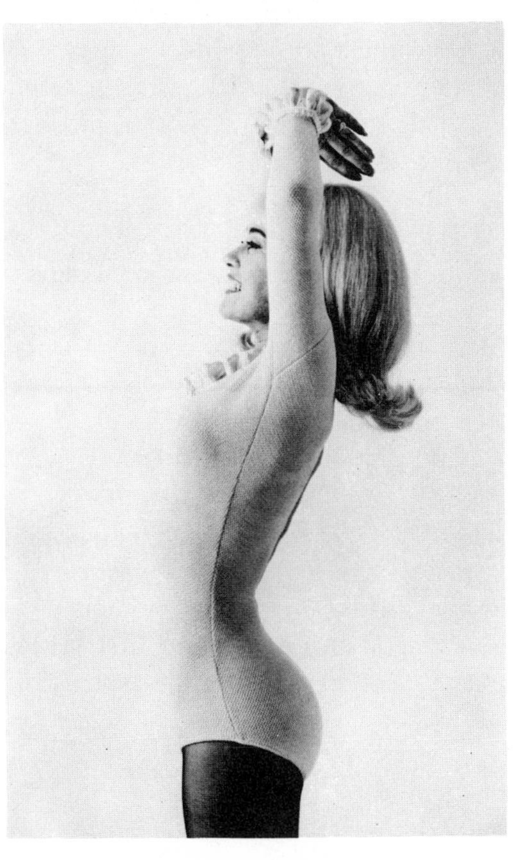

WAISTLINE – LIFELINE

Women of all ages have a tendency toward a protruding tummy. Some women might have a small waistline with very little effort, but a girl with a 24 inch waistline may very easily have a 23 inch waist with the proper form of movement. Sculpturing or molding the body starts as much with the waistline and tummy as any other area. The perfect figure of today is definitely a flat stomach and slim waist. Regardless of what style clothes you may be wearing, the fact that you know it is there can affect you psychologically.

There are over six hundred muscles in your body. They serve many purposes when used. Underdeveloped muscles in the legs, buttocks and arms result in a shapeless, dull figure. When they are not used in the tummy area they allow protrusion. When your muscles are firm in the stomach and waist area you tell the world, without saying a word, that you have pride and are ready for any kind of action. Uncared-for muscles give the appearance of a careless body and mind and undisciplined willpower.

The dancercizes in this chapter are desgined to slim and mold your body to perfection.

Come alive with me and let me take you into the world of complete femininity. Each movement to firm, reduce and contour this area has been designed to give you better results than conventional type exercises because with each one of these you are working on more than one area at once. You are also fulfilling an emotional satisfaction by feeling graceful. In addition, you are educating your body to a variety of movements that will give you poise and gracefulness.

BEAUTY HINTS

1. Do not wear a girdle except with very tight dresses and then only a lightweight one.
2. If you have a small waistline, but would like to take off an extra inch, wear a waist cincher while you are working out. Do not start with it too tight; tighten it as you become accustomed to it.
3. Keep your stomach pulled in and hips tucked under every waking hour.
4. If the style is loose-fitting clothes, don't wear something tight at the waist just to show off your waistline. Helen Gurley Brown, well-known author of *Sex and The Single Girl,* is a perfect example of a well-dressed woman, who has a slim 22 inch waist, but I have yet to see her in anything but the latest fashions, even at the expense of not showing off her tiny waist.

LATIN LOVER (Basic)
Starting position 1. Bend over from the waist with the head up and bounce from the waist.
2. Place your arms in front of your body and circle your arms the entire combination rolling one arm over the other.
3. Lean back from the waist and bounce as you continue your arm motion. Repeat ten times. In sixty days, work up to twenty times.

HALLELUJAH (Basic)

Starting position 1. Standing straight, raise your arms above your head and look up to your hands with your head.

2. Bend over from your waist bringing your arms down between your legs.

3. Swing your arms through your legs and return to starting position.

Do ten times to start, work up to fifteen in thirty days, and thirty by sixty days.

You will find this Dancercize very beneficial and fun to do.

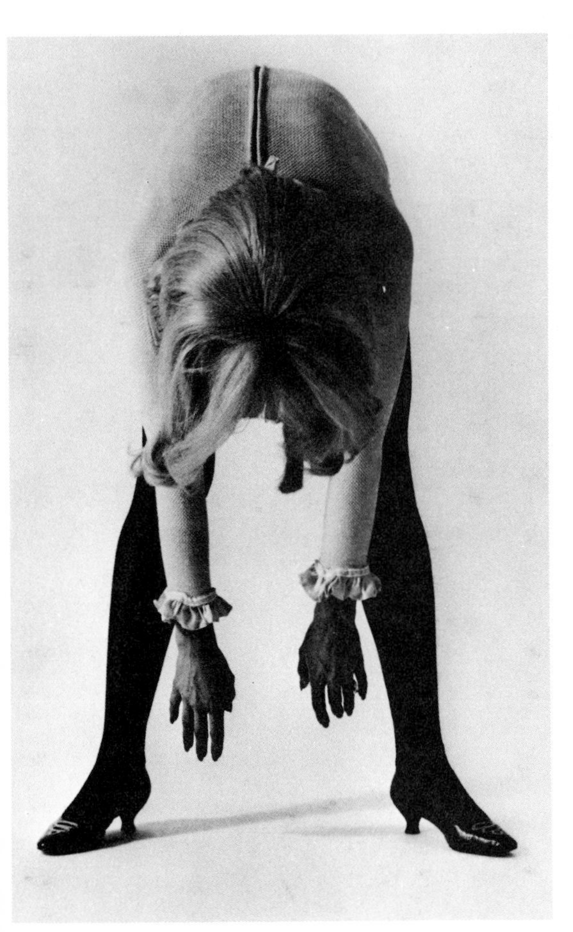

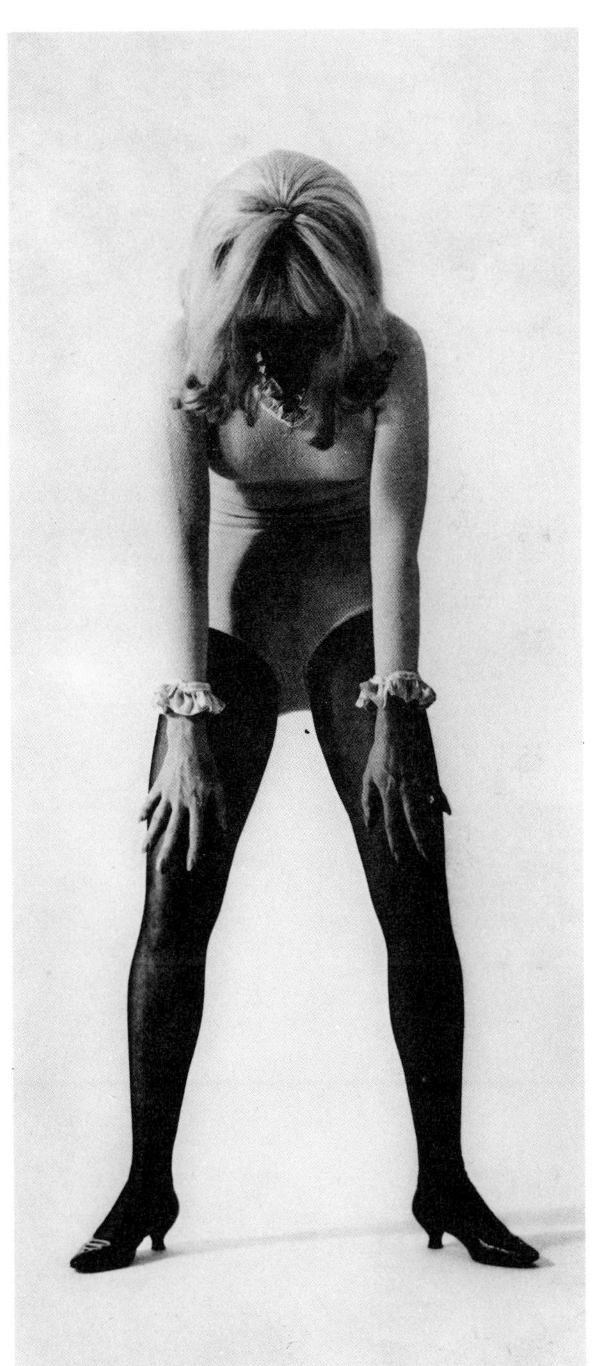

SEXY RELAXICISOR (Beginning)

Starting position 1. Stand straight forward and place your arms down in front of your thighs and keep your head tall.

2. Slowly bend over to the floor, rounding your back and limply relax.

3. Very sluggishly start bringing your body up to starting position, keeping your back rounded and your head still down.

4. Return to starting position by straightening your legs, back and your head.

Do ten times to start, work up to fifteen times in thirty days, and thirty times in sixty days.

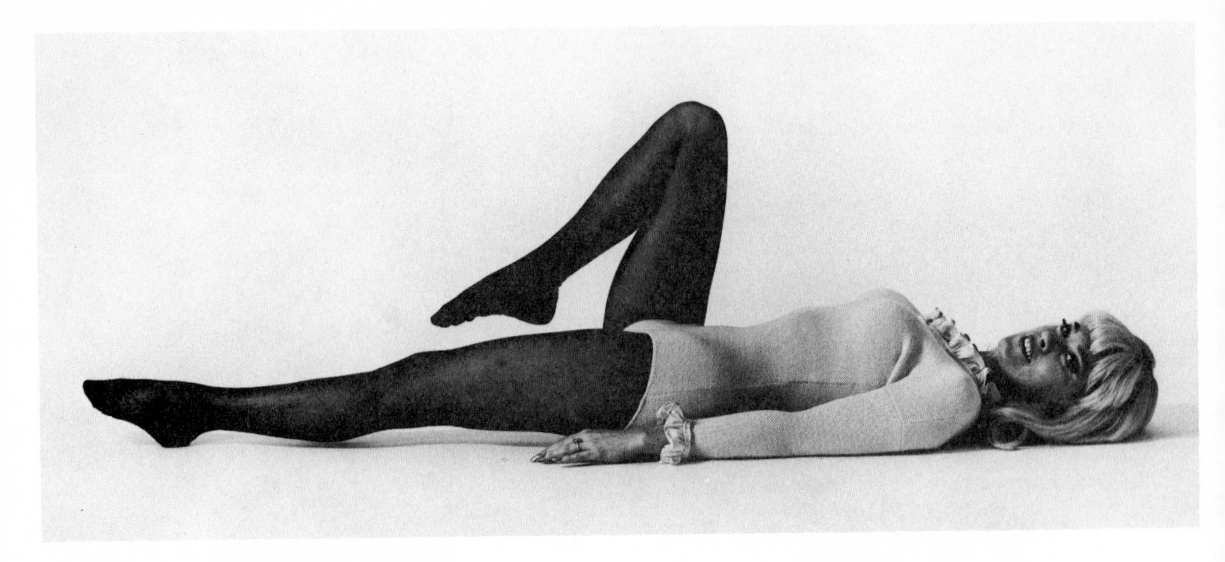

CHALLENGE TO THE TUMMY (Beginning)
Starting position 1. Lie flat on your back with your arms down at your sides. Bend your right knee in, touching your right foot on your left thigh.
2. Straighten your right leg up in the air until you feel a pull.
3. Return to starting position, and repeat on the other leg. Start out doing this Dancercize ten times, within sixty days work up to twenty.

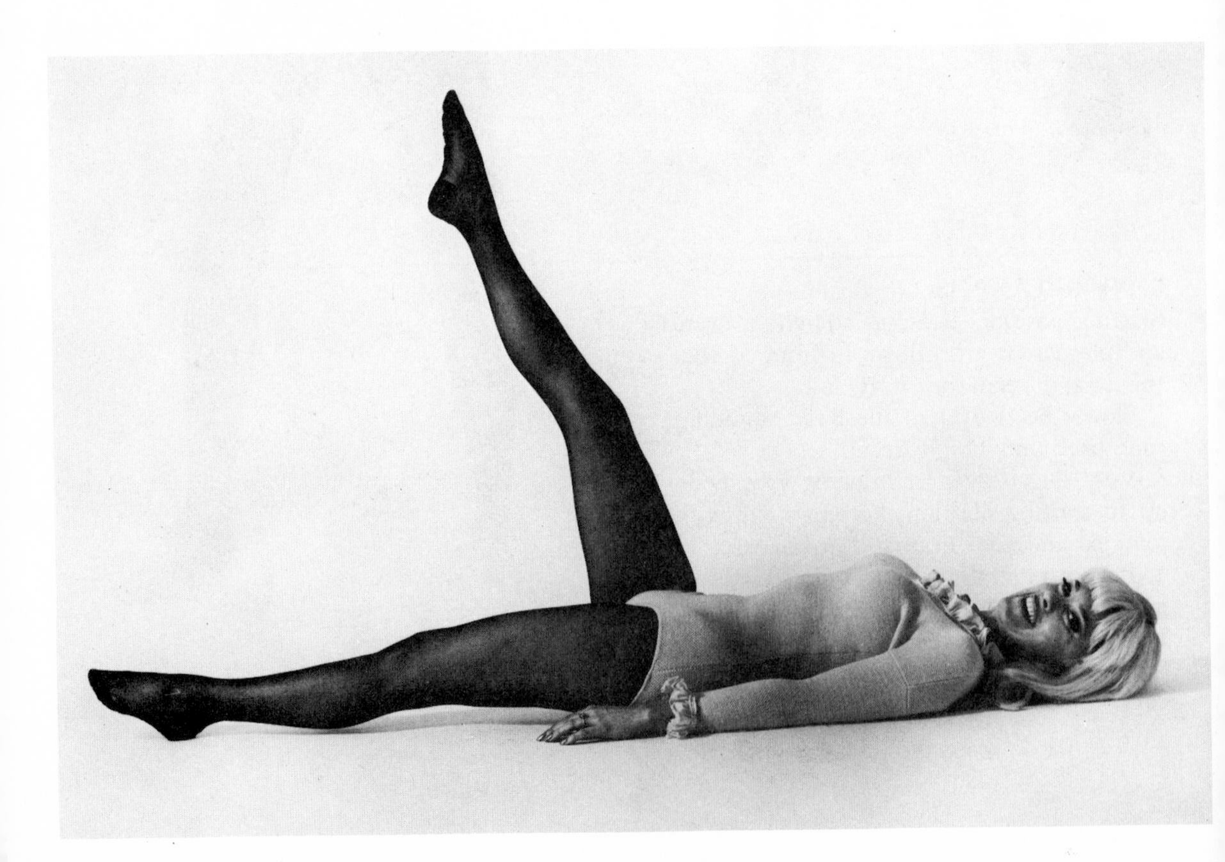

THE STRETCH (Beginning)

Starting position 1. Standing tall with feet apart and head held high, place arms overhead. (Tighten hips and pull in your stomach.)

2. Shift your weight to your right leg and s-t-r-e-t-c-h up to the ceiling with your right arm. Stretch until you reach your final control point.

3. Repeat to the left. Practice shifting your weight until you have the ability to shift quickly and smoothly from one foot to the other.

Do ten to start with. Work up to fifteen in thirty days, and in sixty days you should be doing thirty.

FANCY FELINE (Beginning)

Starting position 1. Begin with weight on right leg, left leg extended back and rigid with left toe pointed.

2. Extend left arm out in front.

3. Elevate your left leg, bending your left knee. Bring your left foot to your right knee with a tight foot.

4. Twist your waist so that your right arm is in front and your left arm extended back.

5. Repeat to the other side after you have done this Dancercize eight times on one leg.

SHOULDER SHIMMY (Beginning)

Starting position 1. Stand straight, legs apart, arms down at sides.

2. Begin bending to the floor.

3. Shimmy your shoulders from your back muscles. (Bringing one arm a little out in front of the other at a time.)

4. Continue shimmying your shoulders from your back muscles until you touch the floor with your fingertips.

5. Return to starting position while you continue the shoulder shimmy and bring your arms out in front at arms level.

6. Bend back from your hips and thighs, bending your legs and continuing your shoulder shimmy. Do ten times to start, work up to fifteen times in thirty days, and thirty times in sixty days.

I'M A BIG GIRL NOW (Beginning)
Starting position 1. Rest hands on waist, legs apart. Keep your head tall.
2. Lean back from hips and thighs, and bounce.
3. Lean forward from waist and bounce. Do ten times to start, work up to fifteen times in thirty days, and thirty in sixty days.

STEP INTO MY PARLOR (Intermediate)
Starting position 1. Stand tall with legs separated.
2. Clasp your hands behind your head, keeping elbows up.
3. Keeping your upper torso quiet, move just your hips to the right. Use motion with control.
4. Return to starting position and repeat to the other side. Do ten times to start, work up to fifteen times in thirty days, and thirty times in sixty days.

GROW-PLAY (Intermediate)
Starting position 1. Sit on floor. Bend your right knee in with your right foot touching your right leg.
2. Bend your left leg to the back.
3. Sit up straight and clap your hands together.
4. Lean to the left and place your left elbow on the floor.
5. Return to starting position, and clap hands.
6. Repeat to the left, clapping hands in between reaching the final control point. Do ten times to start, work up to fifteen in thirty days, and thirty times in sixty days.

FLOOR TOUCH
(Intermediate)
Starting position 1. Start upright, with legs apart, weight slightly on left leg. Raise arms above head.
2. Shift your weight to your right leg. Bend from the waist, touching your hand to your right toe.
3. Return to starting position and repeat eight times. Reverse on other side eight times.

BODY TWIST (Intermediate)
Starting position 1. Stand exalted, place your arms out at your sides and your legs apart.
2. Twist your upper body and turn to the right.
3. Bend from your hips, keeping your back straight and your arms out at your sides.
4. Return to starting position as in 1.
5. Bend forward from your hips, keeping your back level. Keep your arms out to the side and your head up.
6. Return to starting position and repeat to the left.
Do ten times to start, work up to fifteen in thirty days, and thirty by sixty days.

BODY AND LEG TWIST (Intermediate)
Starting position 1. Stand perpendicular, legs apart and arms out at sides. Firm thighs and hips.
2. Turn (twist) your torso and legs to the left and raise your right heel off the floor keeping your weight on your left leg.
3. Place your weight on both of your legs and bend over from your hips. Keep tummy pulled in. Keep your head up and your arms out to the sides.
4. Return to starting position and repeat to the side. Do ten times to start, work up to fifteen in thirty days, and thirty by sixty days.

APPEALING SWING (Intermediate)

Starting position 1. Stand erect with legs apart. Keep your tummy tucked in and hips under.

2. Raise your arms up to the right side (as shown in picture) stretching arms.

3. Head front and held tall.

4. With a continuous motion, begin your swing by stretching way up to the ceiling with your arms (feeling a pull all of the way down your torso).

5. Shift your weight to the right leg, continuing your movement.

6. Make a circle with your body and arms from the side down to the floor.

7. Continue the circle swing of your body over to the left side and come all the way up, making a complete circle with your body and arms until you end up in starting position.

Repeat this Dancercize ten times and work up to twenty times in sixty days.

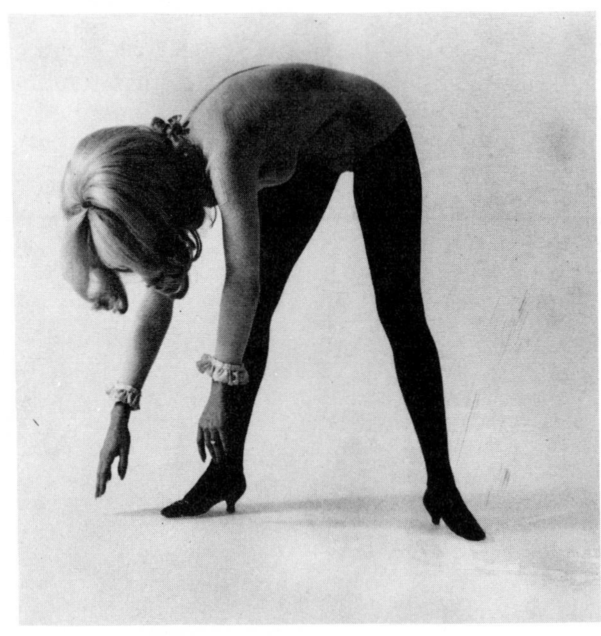

STOMACH PUNCH (Advanced)
Starting position 1. Stand uplifted, place your arms out to the sides.
2. Point your right toe slightly, keep your head up. Your knees should be softly bent.
3. With an explosive movement and impact, imagine that someone hits you in the stomach as you contract or draw in, as you round your back and bring your hands into your stomach. Keep knees softly bent.
4. Return to starting position. Do ten times to start, work up to fifteen times in thirty days, and thirty in sixty days.

THE BUILDUP (Advanced)
Starting position 1. Place your feet apart, knees slightly bent.
2. Bend back from pelvis and bounce four times.
3. Keeping your knees slightly bent, bend over from your waist, and keep your legs apart and your head up.
4. Touch your fingertips to the floor. Return to starting position, and repeat eight more times.

THE PULL (Advanced)
Starting position 1. Stand with your feet apart and turn your body slightly to the left. Place your right hand on your waist and stretch your left arm up to the ceiling.
2. Keeping your legs unbent, bend over, grabbing your left ankle with your right arm. Touch your head to your left knee.
3. Return to starting position and repeat to the other side.
Do ten times to start, work up to fifteen in thirty days, and thirty by sixty days.

STRETCHING IN MOTION (Advanced)
Starting position 1. Arms out to sides, stand tall.
2. Keep left arm out at side.
3. Lean to the left from your waist.
4. Bring your right arm over your head.
5. Continue circling your right arm, bringing it in front of your body even with your left arm.
6. Put your weight on your right leg, bending your right knee.
7. Continue the circle of your right arm until you return to starting position.
Repeat eight times.
Repeat eight times on the other side.

SEDUCTIVE SHIMMY (Advanced)
Starting position 1. Begin by sitting up very tall, head erect and legs straight out in front of you.
2. Stretch arms out in front of you with your palms up.
3. Slowly begin to lie down on the floor. As you go down, shimmy using your back muscles and bringing one arm farther out front at a time. (This is *not* a shoulder shimmy, you use the back muscles for the "Seductive Shimmy.")
4. Now that you are lying down on the floor, slowly start to sit up by raising the body to sitting position. Continue your shimmy throughout this entire Dancercize. You should feel the pull on your stomach muscles as you go up and down.

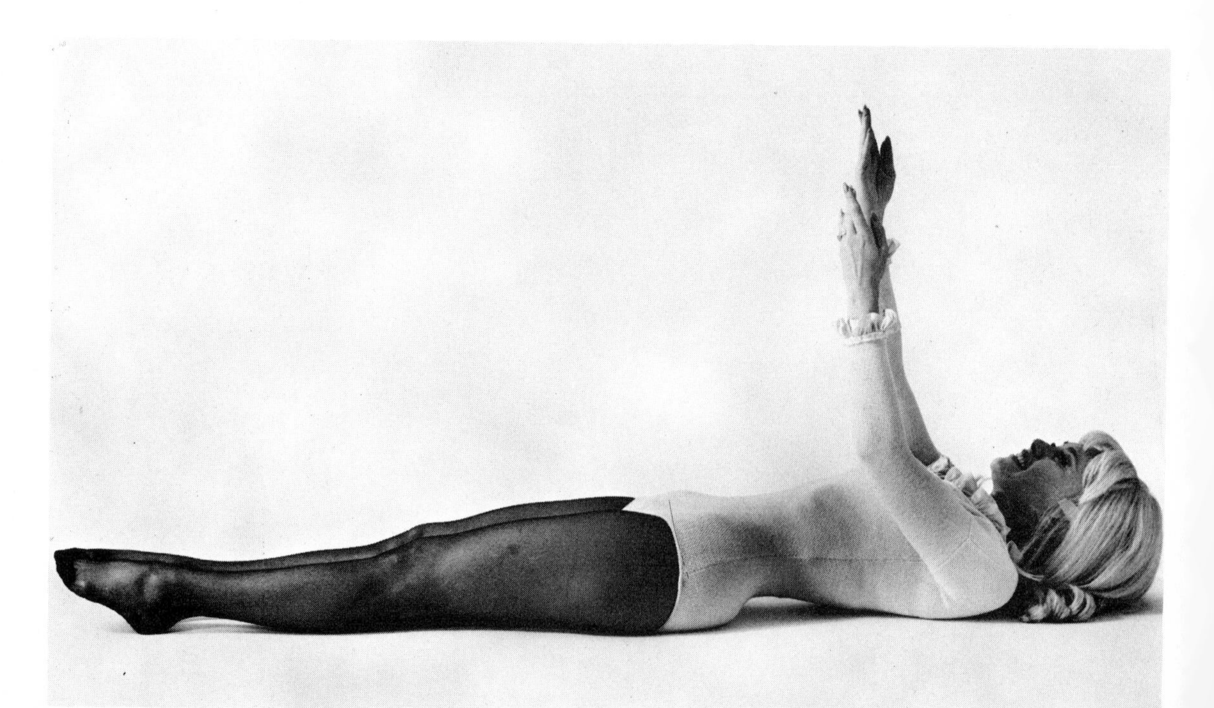

PERFECTING THE PELVIS

One of New York's best photographers, Richard Hochman, told me that any woman looks dead or lifeless without a little movement of the pelvis. This means in everyday life as well as photography. All models know how to tilt the pelvis to add appeal to the clothes they are exhibiting. You should do no less for what you wear.

By perfecting the pelvis movements I give, you will be able to have a controlled tilt instead of a slouch. You will also find you are able to walk with a controlled feminine movement instead of a relaxed wobble or uncontrolled swing. Perfecting this movement will give you more sexy appeal and make you a better love mate.

PELVIS ROCK (Basic)
Starting position 1. Stand tall, place your feet slightly apart and your elbows out. Be sure you keep your head high. Place your fingertips on your rib cage.
2. Thrust your pelvis forward, letting your knees bend.
3. Retain stillness in your entire upper body and rib cage.
4. Return to starting position as shown in No. 1.
Repeat seven times more.

PELVIS ROCK AND ROLL
(Beginning)
Starting position 1. Stand with feet apart, hands on hips.
2. Bend from the waist, keeping your legs straight. Hold your head up and round your back, pulling your pelvis forward.
3. Remain in above position, and straighten your back, pushing your pelvis back and up. Repeat four more times. Work up to twenty within sixty days.

THE CREEP (Beginning)
Starting position 1. Stand with your feet together, head erect. Place one hand on stomach and one hand on your buttocks muscles.
2. Tuck your pelvis under and bend your legs.
3. Remaining in above position, walk around the room. Be sure you keep your legs bent and your pelvis tucked under. Do this ten times. Work up to twenty within sixty days.

AMAZING (Intermediate)
Starting position 1. Watch yourself in the mirror until you have mastered this one. Stand straight as an arrow, place your hands on your rib cage and keep your elbows out, shoulders down, head held high.

2. Hold entire top of body and legs still, move your hips to the right. (Be sure hips move to the side—not back.)

3. Return to starting position and repeat to the left.

4. Repeat seven times more.

FANNY CHIPPER (Intermediate)

Starting position 1. Stand with your legs apart, hands on waist. Keep your back straight and your head erect.

2. Now squat, pushing the pelvis out in back as far as possible.

3. Remain in the squatting position and push your pelvis forward as far as possible.

4. Repeat nine times more.

5. Return to starting position as shown in number one.

6. Continue in the squatting position, and

push your hips and pelvis forward and to the right.

7. Turn your body from the waist, to the right as you push your hips forward to the right.
8. Return to starting position.
9. Still in your squatting position, push your hips forward and to the left.
10. Turn your body from the waist to the left as you push your hips forward to the left.
11. Repeat nine more times.
12. Now do entire combination five times.

HIP AND LEG ROLL (Advanced)
Starting position 1. Stand erect, hands on hips, weight on your right leg.
2. Swing your pelvis and left leg forward.
3. Allowing your pelvis to roll with your leg, bring your left leg and left hip to the left side.
4. Allow your pelvis to roll with your leg, bring your left hip and leg to the back.
5. Repeat three more times.
6. Continue with right leg and hip.

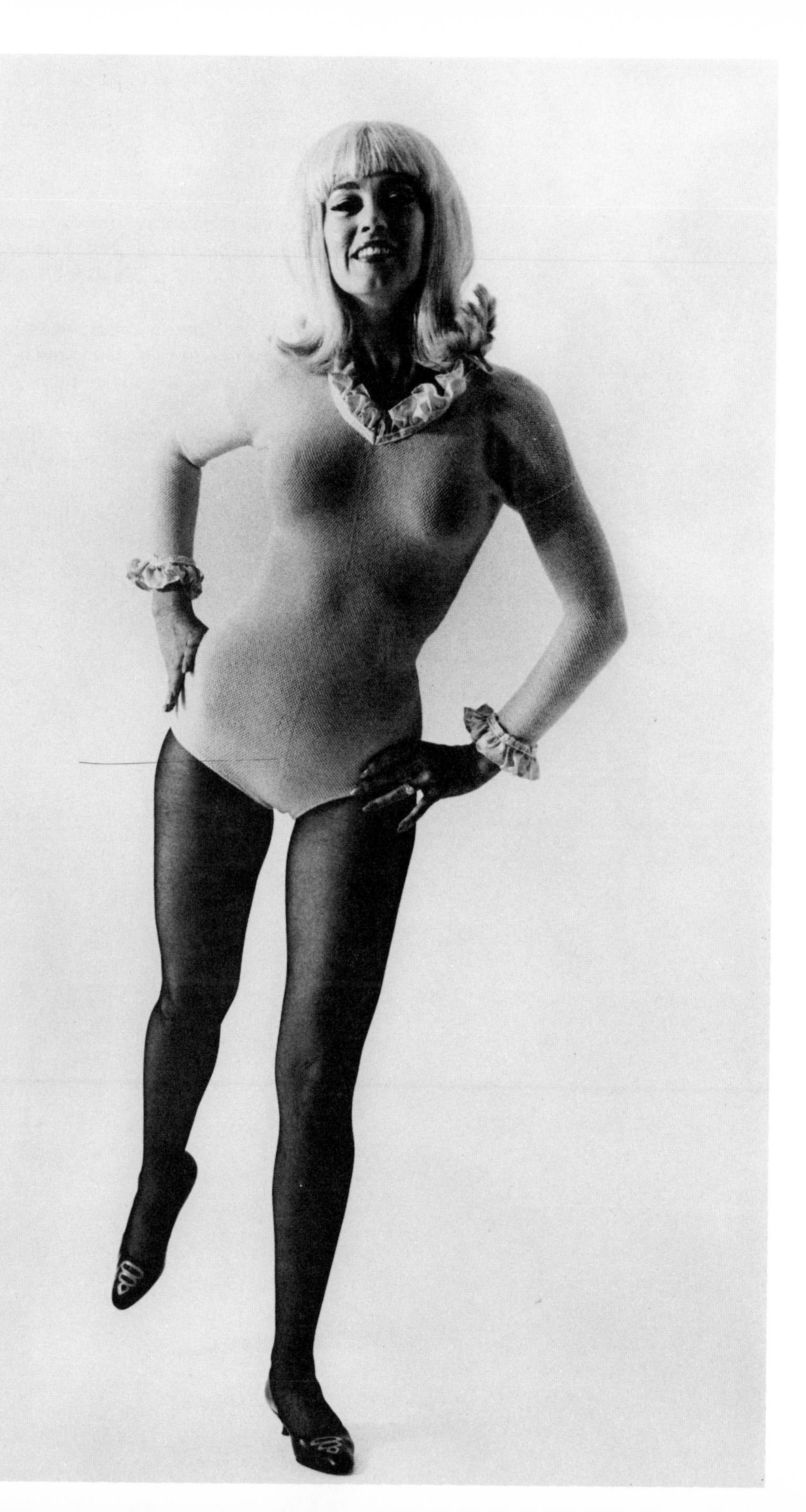

THE SNAKE (Advanced)

Starting position 1. Stand with feet slightly apart, legs straight, hands on hips and head high.

2. Bend over from your hips, keeping your back very straight and your head up. Be sure you don't bend your legs.

3. Carry your body to an upright position, tucking your hips under.

4. Round your back and shoulders and keep your head down.

5. Slow and reverent in mood, bring your head up.

6. Tuck your hips forward, and keep your shoulders slightly rounded.

7. In the same position as above, steadily and harmoniously raise up on your toes, stretching to your fullest height.

8. Repeat three more times.

HIPS AND THIGHS

I have a very dear friend, Beverly Mosko, who is an instructor in the Dancercize clinics I have throughout the country. I wish any woman who has ever felt skepticism or had dubious thoughts about being able to change an overweight plump figure into an attractive slim stylish profile, could meet this charming gal. She would be an inspiration to anyone with a weight problem.

As a young girl she was bulky with unnecessary flesh. At that point in her life she learned, through necessity, how to devise "many a disguise for oversize", as she called them. I have them listed for you at the bottom of the page. While you are in the process of losing weight, and have not as yet achieved your desired goal, these tips will help make you appear slimmer by not calling attention to what you are trying to get rid of.

Today, through diet and Dancercize, Beverly maintains a slender attractive figure. She has traveled as a Jimmy Durante dancer, and has also worked as a Copa Girl in New York. Her wardrobe now includes bright colors, polka dots, stripes, all the striking things a tall slim girl can wear.

Some women consider a fashionable derriere one that is flattened by a girdle with no movement and no shape, but it is a far cry from the opinions of men, including doctors. Much can be done to mold the buttocks into a shapely, youthful form without the aid of anything but determination, willpower and proper movements to shape and firm the muscles. A lazy set of buttocks (flabby ones that can't be controlled when you walk) can be one of the most unattractive parts of the female anatomy. On the other hand, if your hips are firm and have been developed properly they will compete with your bust and legs in contributing to sex appeal.

BEAUTY TIPS

Until you have figure perfection, here are some suggestions that might be helpful in disguising large hips.

1. Never wear light colors from the waist down.
2. Colored shoes, including white, should only be worn in the evening. Colored shoes draw attention to the lower part of the body.
3. Don't wear clothes with pockets.
4. Floral prints, stripes in either direction, polka dots or anything with a large or busy pattern tend to make you look larger.
5. A belt another color than your dress cuts the illusion in the middle and makes the hips look larger.
6. Gathered and pleated skirts are out.

7. Three-quarter-length sleeves also make your hips look larger when your arms are down at your sides. It is best to wear sleeves long or above the elbow.
8. When standing don't rest your hands on your hips.
9. Stretch pants are out unless they are a dark color and fit well. There are many cute three-quarter overblouses you can wear with slacks that camouflage the hips.
10. NEVER wear bermudas or short shorts in public.
11. Needless to say, no bikinis or two-piece bathing suits. It is more flattering to a heavy figure to wear bathing suits with a boy-cut leg.
12. In wearing a plain dress, be sure you don't select one with any pattern (no matter how small) around the hips.

THE WALK (Basic)
Everyone knows that walking is good for you, but in order to derive all of the benefits, you must walk correctly. In this Dancercize we are going to walk around the room, exaggerating every movement in order to work every muscle.
Starting position 1. Place your weight on your left foot.
2. Right foot back resting lightly on your toes.
3. Your right arm is front and your left arm back, hold your head high and keep your shoulders down.
4. Place your right foot in front of your left and change your arms.
5. Now, shift your weight so that your weight is on your right foot and your left foot is pointed back.
6. Walk briskly around the room at least twenty times.

DUTCH KICKS (Basic)
Starting position 1. Stand tall with your feet together, place your hands on your hips.
2. Raise your left foot back off of the floor, bending at the knee, and be sure to point your toe.
3. Kick your left leg straight front with stamina as you flex your foot (bend toes up).
4. Return to starting position and repeat to the right. Do this ten times, and work up to twenty within sixty days.

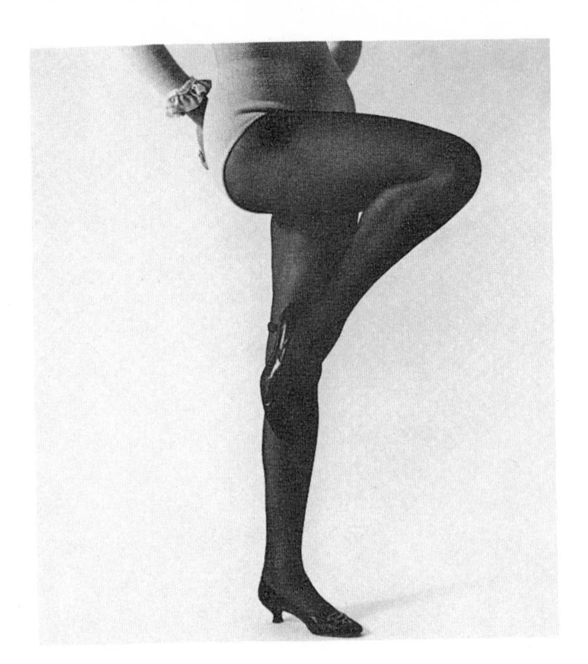

COZ (Basic)

Starting position 1. Stand with your hands behind your back and with straight legs, point your left foot back with form and place your weight on your right leg.
2. Raise your right knee up in front until your right foot touches your left knee.
3. Return to starting position and repeat four times more. Repeat on other leg four times. Work up to doing this twenty times in sixty days.

THE FROG (Beginning)

Starting position 1. Lie on your stomach with your head and shoulders off the floor.
2. Take your legs out to the sides raising them a little off the floor.
3. Return to starting position.
4. Kick your right leg up in back, keeping your leg straight.
5. Repeat entire combination ten times, kicking your left leg up in back. Within sixty days be doing this Dancercize twenty times.

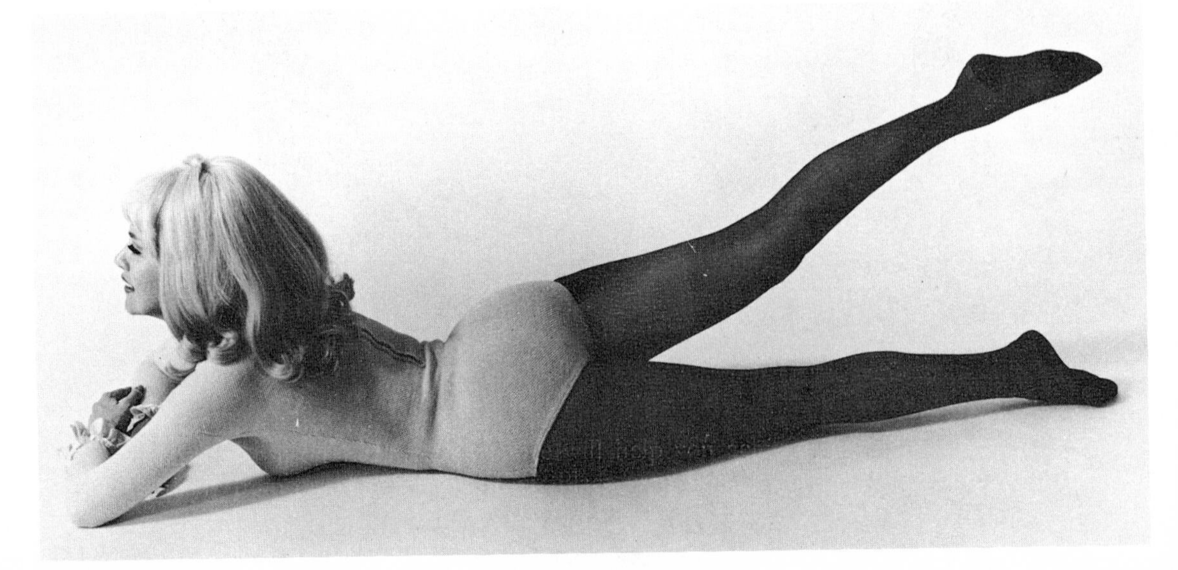

THE ALERT (Beginning)
Starting position 1. Now that I have you walking around the room, why stop? Try this one. Head and body erect and your feet together on the floor.
2. Keeping your left foot flat on the floor, raise your right knee up.
3. Put your left arm in front and your right arm back and twist your body at the waist so that your left arm is in front of your right knee.
4. Repeat on the other foot and walk around the room at least twenty times.

BODY STRETCH
Starting position 1. Stand tall, head front. Raise your left arm up to the ceiling and your right arm straight back.
2. Raise your left leg straight back off the floor and st-r-e-t-c-h.
3. Walk around the room doing this Dancercize, alternating legs. Create a graceful form for this one. Do eight times to start, and work up to twenty times in sixty days.

KNEE TWIST (Beginning)
Starting position 1. Stand tall, head facing front. Keep your shoulders down and place your arms out to the sides.
2. Raise your left knee up, touching your left foot to the right leg.
3. Staying in same position as above, twist your left knee in.
4. Remaining in the same position, twist your left knee out.
5. Return to starting position. Repeat four times on each leg.
Work up to twenty times in sixty days.

STOMACH LEVELER (Basic)
(Beginning)

Starting position 1. Stand tall with your head forward. Keep your left arm down and your right arm up to the ceiling, turning your right palm back.

2. Raise your right foot to your left knee.

3. Lean your body a little forward and lean to the right.

4. Return to starting position.

5. Repeat on the other side.

Do ten times, and work up to twenty in sixty days.

FRONT KICKS (Beginning)
Starting position 1. This Dancercize will help you achieve the ability to shift quickly from one foot to the other. Place your right leg behind your left and rest your weight on the ball of your right foot.
2. Left leg remains straight and your arms out to the sides.
3. Bend your right knee, keeping your foot back.

4. Kick your right leg straight front with power.
5. Return to starting position.
6. Repeat seven times more and then repeat on other leg. (This Dancercize is also very good for flabby knees.) Do eight times and work up to twenty within sixty days.

BENT KICKS (Beginning)
Starting position 1. Stand tall with your arms out at the sides, head up.
2. Place your weight on your left leg.
3. Place your right leg behind your left, and rest on the ball of your right foot.
4. Raise your right knee as high as possible.
5. Return to starting position.
6. Repeat to the other side. (It might be a good idea to hold on to a wall or a chair until you master this one.) Do ten times and work up to twenty in sixty days.

GO-GO-GO (Beginning)

Knee bounces are an excellent and fun way to firm and reduce the hip, thigh and buttock muscles. There are many various ways to do knee bounces, as you will see in the next seven Dancercizes.

Starting position 1. Stand tall, legs straight, arms out to the sides and your shoulders down, head at full tilt.

2. Keep knees together and arms out, bounce knees to the left side. Be sure to keep your knees together.

3. Return to starting position.

4. Bounce knees to the right side four times.

5. Repeat combination nine more times.

LARIAT (Intermediate)
Starting position 1. Stand with your feet together, place your right hand up in the air and pretend you are a sexy cowgirl holding a lariat. Place your left hand down at your side.
2. Keeping the same position, begin to circle your arm with enthusiasm (twirling your lariat) and bounce your knees. Now go on, "sexy cowgirl"—ride.

CHARLESTON ANYONE?

(Intermediate)

Starting position 1. Stand upright, clasp your fingers together with your palms down.

2. Elevate your right knee front, as high as possible, and hit your hands on your right knee.

3. Return to starting position.

4. Hit your right knee four times and repeat on the left.

Do this ten times to start, and work up to twenty within sixty days.

BACK BOUNCE (Intermediate)
Starting position 1. Stand erect, arms out to the sides. Place your right foot front, and your left leg in back of the right, feet apart.
2. Lean back from hips, bending your left leg and bounce four times.
3. Return to starting position.
4. Place your right foot in back of left and repeat, bending your right leg and bouncing.
Do ten times to start, and work up to twenty in sixty days.

IDE BOUNCE (Intermediate)
tarting position 1. Stand tall, face the ght side and place your hands on your ighs. Keep shoulders down and head rect. Legs out to the sides.

. Continue facing the side and bend our right leg and bounce four times.

. Return to starting position.

. Turn to face the left side and repeat he bounce on your left leg.

)o eight to start with, and work up to venty in sixty days.

ON GUARD
(Intermediate)
Starting position 1. Stand perpendicular, legs parted, arms out to sides, shoulders down and head exalted.
2. Retain straightness in your body and bend left leg to the left side and bounce four times.
3. Return to starting position, and repeat to the right. Work up twenty in sixty days.

THE KILLER (Advanced)
Starting position 1. Lie down on your back, bend your knees and place your feet on the floor.
2. Keep your arms down at your sides with the palms of your hands on the floor.
3. Pushing with your pelvis, raise your hips and waist off the floor.
4. Keeping the same position, bend your left knee in to your chest.
5. Still in same position, kick your left leg forward and up.
6. Slowly lower your left leg, keeping your hips and waist off of the floor.
7. Return to starting position and repeat one more time. Repeat with right leg.

ANTENNA UP (Advanced)

Starting position 1. Stand with legs apart and arms out to the sides. Keep your shoulders down and head up.

2. Remain in starting position, and raise up on the balls of your feet.

3. Your heels come off of the floor as you bend your knees. These knee flexes are done with explosive movement.

4. Continue flexing your knees until you can do it easily with control of your motions.

5. Now, as you continue flexing your knees, keep your arms out to the sides and make little circles (forward and around—keeping your shoulders still and down) with your arms.

You will find this Dancercize very helpful for coordination, back and arms.

DEBBIE'S ROCK (Advanced)

Starting position 1. Stand erect, hands on your thighs and legs separated.
2. Point your left toe with intensity.
3. Bringing your left heel off of the floor, lean forward slightly from your waist.
4. Bend your right leg and bounce four times.
5. Shift your body and lean back, keeping the same leg position and bounce four times.
6. Repeat three times more and repeat on the other side four times.
Work up to twenty within sixty days.

HOEDOWN (Advanced)
Starting position 1. Stand with your feet apart, clasp your fingers together and turn your palms down.
2. Keeping your hands still, raise your left knee as high as possible.
3. As you raise your knee, flex your left foot (turn your toes up).
4. Return to starting position.
5. Repeat seven more with your left leg and then repeat with the right. Work up to twenty in sixty days.

PONY WALK

Starting position 1. Stand erect. Raise your left knee as high as possible to your chest.

2. Let your arms swing naturally, bring your right arm front, left arm back.

3. Now alternate legs and arms and walk around the room at least twenty times. Make your movements reach a climax of activity. "Ride, pony, ride."

LEISURE (Advanced)

Starting position 1. Stand erect with arms out to the sides, head up.

2. Place your weight on your right leg and place your left leg behind your right, resting on the ball of your left foot.

3. Raise your left foot with gentle eloquence to right knee.

4. Return to starting position.

Repeat on the other leg. Do ten times to start, and work up to twenty in sixty days.

THE LEGGIER LOOK
OR PUT YOUR BEST FOOT FORWARD

It is not only great fun, but good for your feet to walk on sand in the summer. Curl toes under after you place your foot in the sand (this is an excellent exercise). Go barefoot occasionally, it gives your feet a chance to breath, especially to give them some sunshine.

Feet are primarily bones, and for good bones you need essential nutrition. Strong bones require plenty of calcium (milk and cheese), vitamin C and vitamin D.

"Half of the length and half the weight of your body is legs." You not only want your legs to look shapely, but they have to feel and perform well, too. Contoured legs add infinitely to a woman's beauty. You don't have to be young to have shapely legs. Some of the most famous legs in the world are possessed by those well over twenty-one. Walking, stair climbing and bicycling are some of the best exercises for your legs. So next time, leave your car at home.

A few years ago when I was in Germany I saw Marlene Dietrich doing a nightclub act with dancers in their twenties, perhaps even younger, and not only did her legs look as well as the other girls, but she had the most shapely legs in the entire cast.

If you have thick ankles or unshapely calves, please do not accept defeat until you have worked on this chapter. I've been able to help girls, who felt there was nothing that could be done, slim down ankles. Certainly nothing can be done about bone structure, but many women confuse fat and swelling in the ankle area for thick-bonedness; and it is often hard to discriminate between the two.

Regardless of how good you feel or how healthy you are, if your feet are not in good shape physically, you will show tension in your face and it will make your whole body tired. Dancercize will give strength to the foot and ankle.

BEAUTY HINTS

1. If you are going to wear shorts, and you have uneven pigmentation or spider veins; or you have been a good girl and stayed out of the sun to keep you from aging, you will find leg makeup very flattering to your legs. There are many on the market. Personally I prefer John Robert Powers because it goes on smoothly without streaking.
2. You can use the same leg makeup for shading your ankles and calves. It looks beautiful under hose. There are various ways of shading. To get the best results, when you purchase leg makeup, ask the cosmetologist to show you how to apply it for your particular shape legs.

3. ALWAYS wear hose with a dress.
4. Be sure your hose never bag at the knee. Change brands until you find one that does not bag.
5. Never wear garters. Anything tight around the leg can make spider veins.
6. Never wear an ankle bracelet. Ankle bracelets were panned as being a fashionable accessory. Although they do have a certain amount of sex appeal, do not take a chance of looking out of place; only wear them around the house.
7. Never wear hose with rhinestones.
8. The size heel on your shoes should always be in balance with the length of your dress. If you have a small budget, stick to basic (plain and simple) colors and styles in your shoe wardrobe. This way you will be able to go along with the trend.
9. Don't wear scuffed shoes or worn down heels. You'd be surprised at how many people look at your feet.
10. Ankle hose are much more attractive than bobby socks or bare feet when wearing slacks.

When you have mastered the individual dance steps, you can blend them into any number of popular and original dance steps. The pleasure of moving to music as you follow these exercises will reward you with a supple, healthy body; inner confidence, poise and, no doubt, the X factor which is every woman's birthright—sex appeal. Go to it. And good luck.

STUBBORN (Basic)
Starting position 1. Sit on the floor with a very straight back, and your head held proudly.
2. Bend your right knee and bring foot in.
3. Pull your foot back as far as possible.
4. Return to starting position and repeat with the other leg, do with each leg five times. Work up to twenty times within sixty days.

FEET FLEX (Basic)
Starting position 1. Sit on floor with your legs together, turn your feet out slightly and point your toes with force.
2. Pull your feet back (flex feet) with gusto.
3. Return to starting position.
Repeat ten times, and within sixty days work up to twenty times.

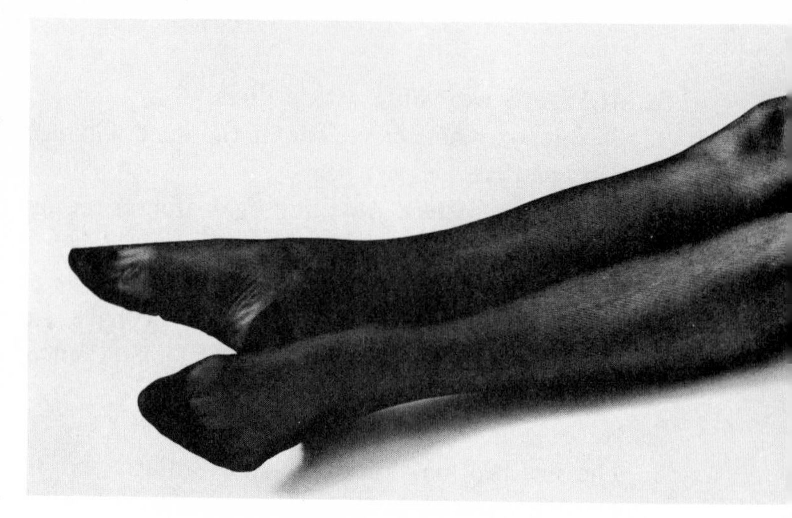

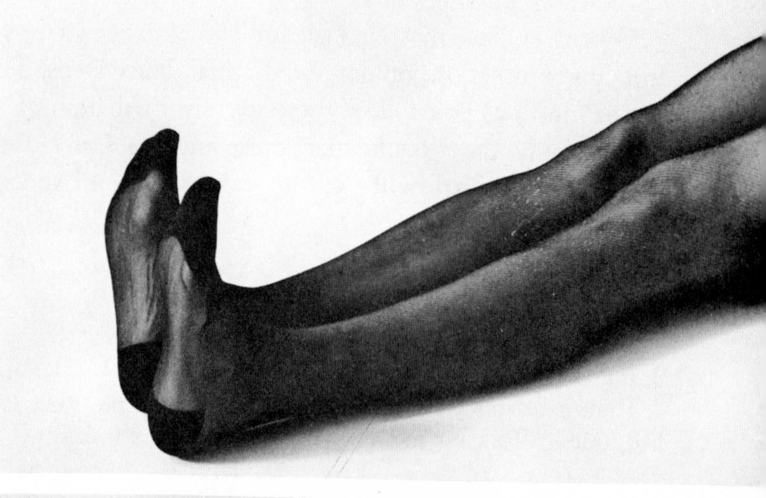

DOUBLE WHAMMY
(Beginning)
Starting position 1. Sit on the floor with your legs together, toes pointed with sharpness.
2. Flex both of your feet, keeping your legs and body still, pulling your feet back as far as possible.
3. Return to starting position, and repeat nine times more.
4. Now, alternate your feet by pointing your right toe and flexing your left foot.
5. Point your left toe and flex your right foot.
Do this ten times to start, and work up to twenty times within sixty days.

DOUBLE PROJECT (Beginning)

Starting position 1. Sit on floor with your legs apart, place your hands on the floor behind your back for support.

2. Keep your head erect, back straight as an arrow, point your toes.

3. At the same time, flex your feet and bend your knees.

4. Return to starting position, and repeat ten more times, work up to twenty times within sixty days.

5. Now, alternate by pointing your right toe, keeping leg straight.

6. Flex your left foot and bend your left knee. Repeat to the other side.

CROSSED SWORDS (Beginning)

Starting position 1. Lying on your back, brace yourself with your hands on your back and lift your legs, hips and back off the floor, so that you are resting your shoulders on the floor.

2. With straight legs, cross your left leg in front of your right leg.

Remaining in the same position, begin bringing your left leg down by bending your left knee.

3. Continue bringing your left leg down until your left foot is on your right thigh.

4. Return to starting position and repeat with the other leg. Repeat this ten times, and work up to twenty times within sixty days.

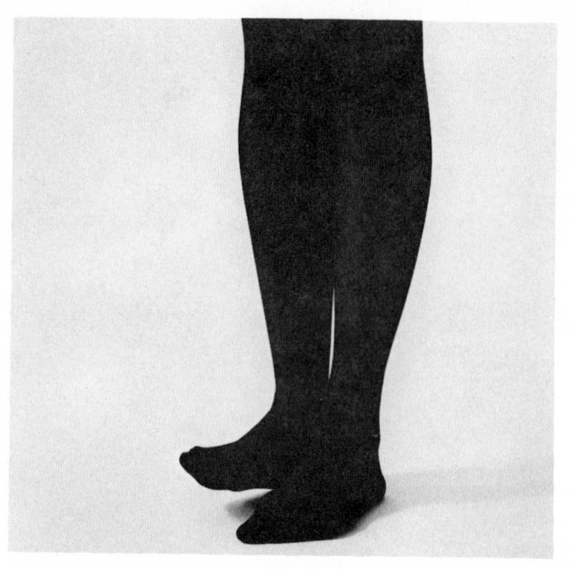

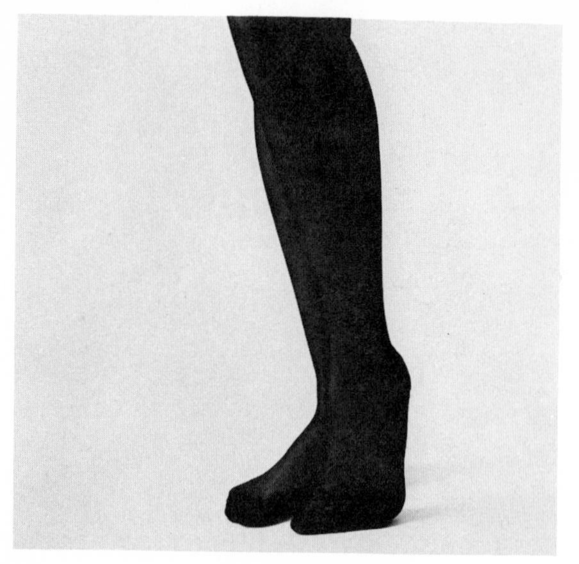

TOE, TOE, HEEL, HEEL (Beginning)

Starting position 1. Stand erect with your feet together.
2. While the rest of your body remains still, raise your right toes off of the floor.
3. Return to starting position.
4. Raise your left toes off of the floor.
5. Alternate with right toes, left toes ten times.
6. With toes remaining on the floor, raise your left heel off the floor.
7. Return to starting position, and raise your right heel off the floor.
8. Alternate, raising your left heel then right heel off the floor ten times.
9. Raise up on both toes.
10. Return to starting position ten times.
11. Keeping your heels on the floor, raise both toes off the floor and return to starting position.
12. Now combine the last two movements, alternating up on your toes, return to starting position.
13. Heels on the floor, toes off of the floor.
14. Return to starting position. Do this ten times to start, and work up to twenty times within thirty days.

You will feel this working on your calves, as well as all other parts of your legs, ankles and feet.

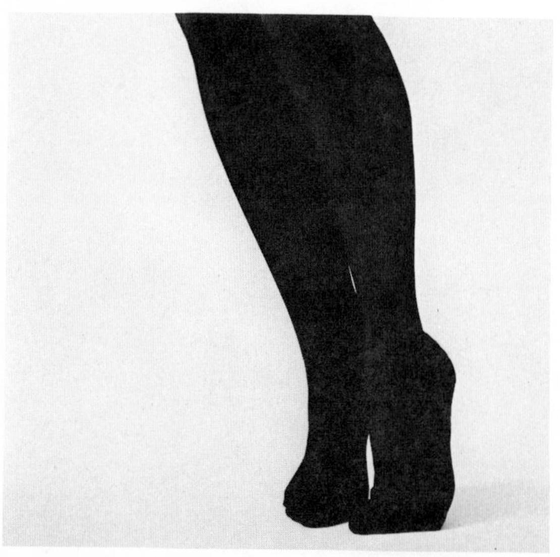

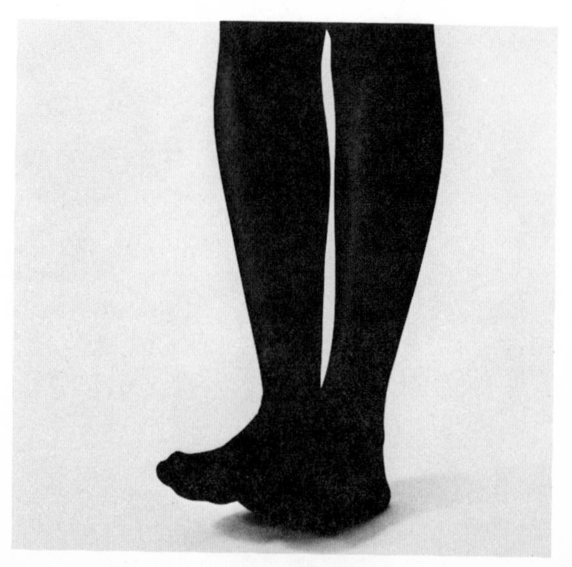

DELICATE BACK POINT (Beginning)
Starting position 1. With legs straight and body rigid, place your feet together.
2. Keeping your body inflexible, and buttocks muscles tucked under, point your left foot back with a tight foot, moving your leg from your hip socket.
3. Return to starting position, moving leg from the hip socket.
4. Repeat four times with each leg.
Within sixty days work up to doing this twenty times.

CLASSY FOOT CIRCLE
Starting position 1. This can also be done sitting down, while watching television, etc. Stand tall with your hands on your hips, legs straight.
2. Raise your left leg in front and make a complete circle with your right foot starting clockwise.
3. Circle ten times.
4. Circle your left foot ten times.
5. Start with your right foot again and circle counterclockwise ten times.
6. Repeat with your left foot.
Within sixty days you should be able to do this twenty times.

FLOOR KICK (Intermediate)
Starting position 1. Lie on your right side and support yourself with your right arm.
2. Keeping your right leg straight and on the floor, bend your left leg until your left toes are even with your right knee.
3. Kick your left leg up in the air at 45° angle, keeping it straight.
4. Repeat to the other side. Do this five times on each side.

BRISKY BRUSH (Intermediate)
Starting position 1. Start with your right foot in front of your left, with weight on your left leg.
2. With gusto, brush the right leg back off the floor, brushing the ball of your right foot.
3. Return to starting position, and repeat to the other side.
Do this ten times to start with, work up to twenty in sixty days.

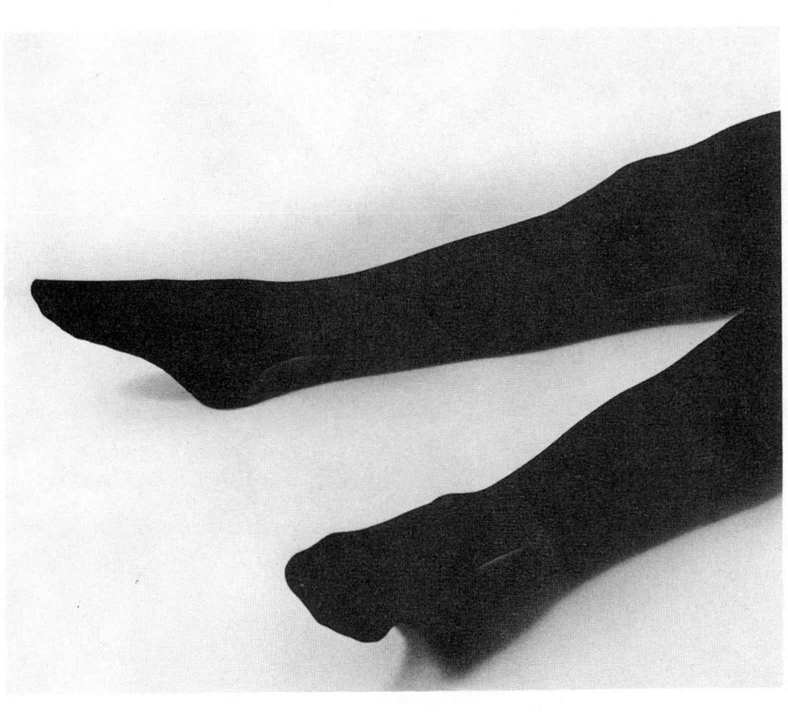

TECHNIQUE
(Intermediate)

Starting position 1. Sitting on floor, place your legs slightly apart, point your toes straight front.
2. Keeping your toes pointed, with control, turn just your feet out.
3. Flex your feet, pulling your feet back as far as possible.
4. Return to starting position, and repeat ten times. Within thirty days work up to doing this twenty times.

DELICATE FRONT POINT (Intermediate)

Starting position 1. Stand erect, toes turned slightly out.
2. Begin to point right toe front, keeping your right leg straight and moving from your hip socket.
3. Point your right toe straight front.
4. Return to starting position.
5. Repeat five times with each leg. Start out doing this ten times, work up to twenty in sixty days.

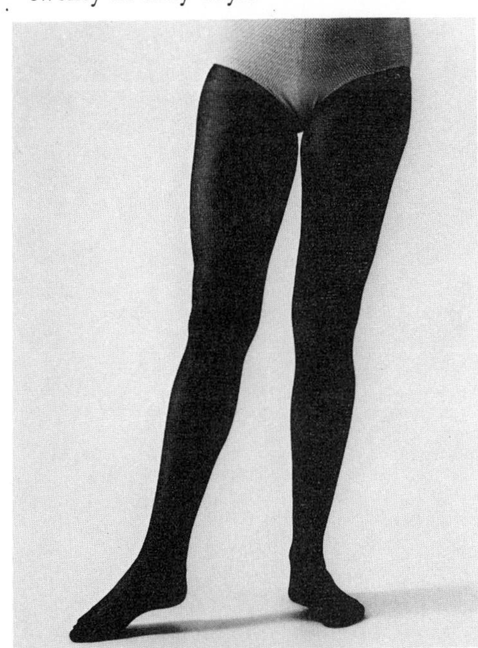

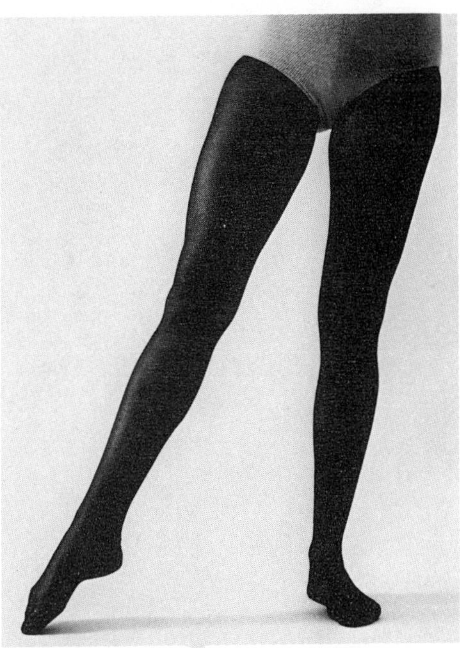

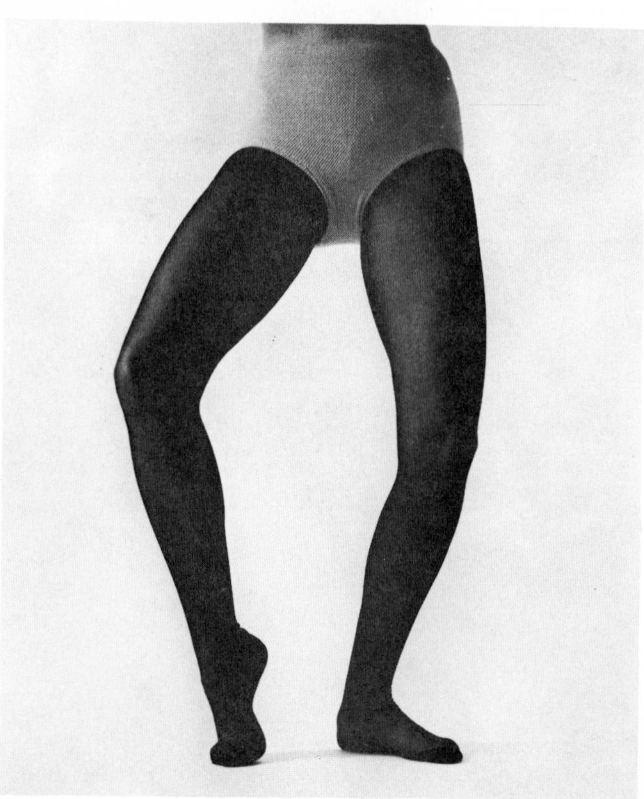

FANCY FOOT FLEX

(Intermediate)

Starting position 1. Stand with feet turned slightly out, hands on chest, knees bent.

2. Keep knees bent and the same starting position. Raise up on the ball of your left foot. (Your weight stays evenly distributed.)

3. Now, try it with your other foot.

4. Alternate your feet ten times, returning to starting position each time.

5. Raise up on the balls of both your feet and return to starting position ten times. Be sure to keep your body and hips still. Work up to doing this twenty times within sixty days.

HILLBILLY BOUNCE (Advanced)
Starting position 1. Raise body tall, with hands down at your sides. Straighten your arms rigidly with fingers stretched.
2. Bend your right knee.
3. Place your left leg, stretched straight, as far front as possible.
4. Raise your left knee up, foot flexed.
5. Bounce on your right leg (bent—straight).
6. Bending your right leg, place your left heel on the floor stretched straight front as far as possible.
7. Now, repeat raising your left knee up, foot flexed, and bounce on your right leg. Do this five times on each leg.

HIGHLAND FLING (Advanced)
Starting position 1. Stand tall with your left leg straight, place your right leg in front, straight and raised off floor.
2. Cross your left foot in front of your right and tap your right toe on the floor.
3. Return to starting position.
4. Cross your left foot behind your right leg and tap your left toe on the floor.
5. Repeat four times more and then change to right foot.

The following jumps are great for heart stimulation and for legs, calves, ankles and feet. When you jump, try to keep your body still and only work your legs and feet. Start all jumps by first taking your heels off the floor, then the ball of the foot; toes come off last. When returning to the floor, land toes, ball of foot, heel. ALWAYS be sure to bend your legs before and after any jump.

JUMP CHANGE
Starting position 1. Place the weight on your right foot, left leg bent back and out slightly to the side.
2. Now, jump onto your left foot, bringing your right foot bent back and slightly out to the side.
Start out doing this ten times, work up to twenty in sixty days.

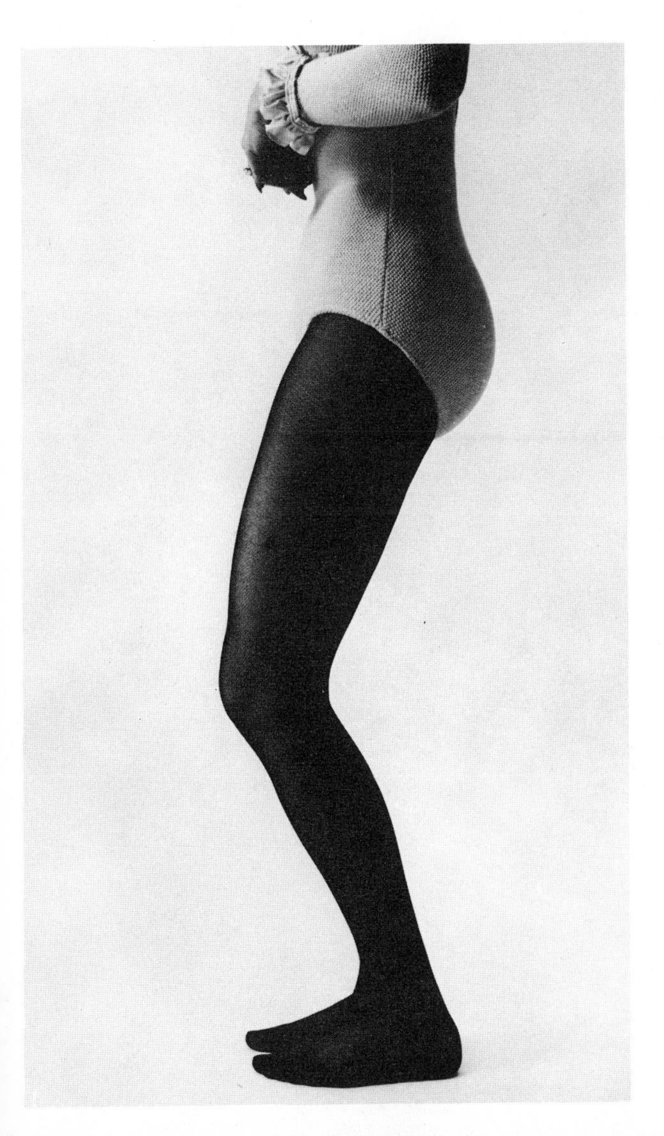

TOGETHER JUMP
(Advanced)
Starting position 1. Legs together, feet turned slightly out, legs bent and body straight.
2. Spring off the floor, straightening your legs and pointing your toes.

CAN CAN (Advanced)
Starting position 1. Stand with weight on your slightly bent right leg.
2. Bend your left leg.
3. With your left foot at your right knee.
4. Begin to raise and straighten your left leg in front.
5. Straighten your left leg off the floor and in front of you.
6. Return to starting position as shown in No. 1 and repeat nine times more.
7. Reverse to the other leg.
8. With your weight on your right leg, bend your left knee as high as possible.
9. Kick your left leg out and across your right leg, keeping your body straight front.
10. Return to starting position, and repeat nine more times.
11. Reverse to the other side.
12. After you have mastered this Dancercize, then try one kick straight front and then one cross kick. Remember to always return to starting position.
To make it more fun you might try a little hop on your right foot every time you kick your leg and when you bend it in—"Happy Can Can."

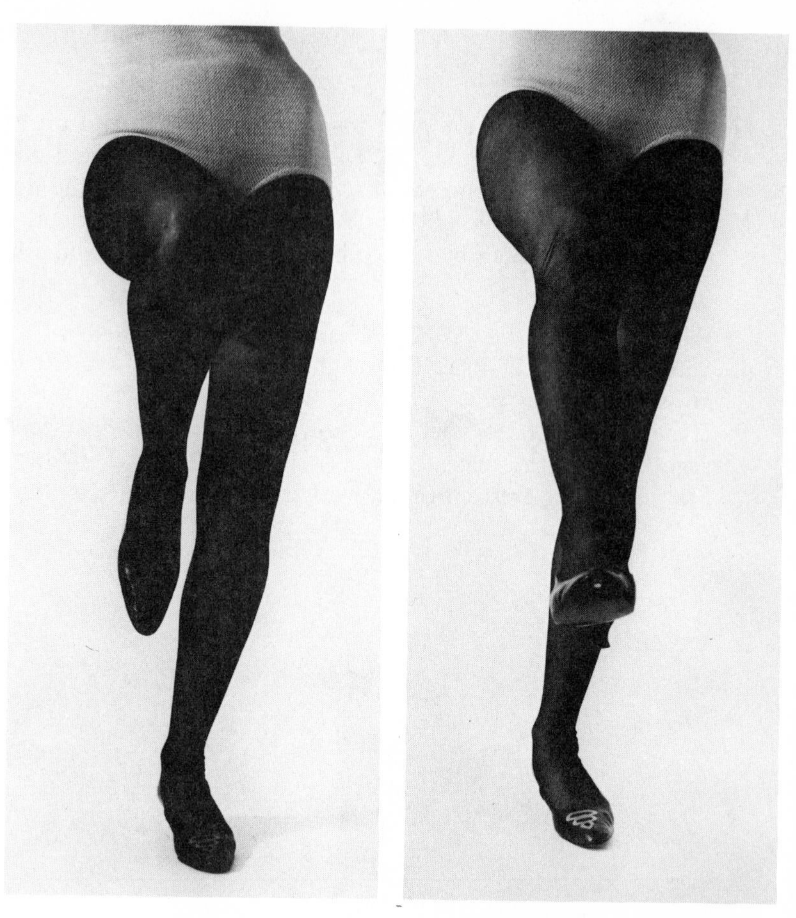

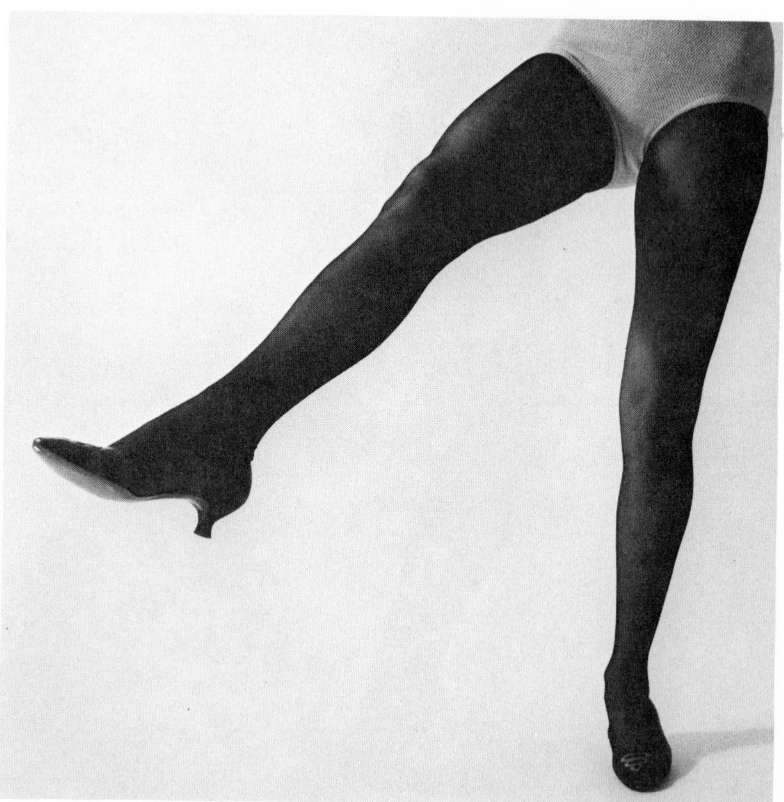

APART JUMPS (Advanced)
Starting position 1. Body straight, legs apart, legs bent, weight evenly distributed on both feet.
2. Spring off the floor, straightening your legs and pointing your toes.
Do this ten times to start, work up to twenty times in sixty days.

PRETTY PONY

Starting position 1. Kneel on the floor, with fists clenched, extend your arms straightforward. (Don't bend elbows.)

2. With straight arms and your body in line with your arms, keep your back straight and move your torso from the waist up to the right.

3. Stay in this position and pulse (bounce) the body three times.

4. Return to starting position, repeat to the other side.

Repeat entire combination ten times. Work up to doing it twenty times within sixty days.

TIPSY TOE TOUCH

Starting position 1. Stand tall with the legs slightly apart.

2. Raise your right arm above your head.

3. Bend your right leg in back of your left and touch your left fingertips to the right foot, leaning to the left from the waist.

4. Return to starting position, and repeat on the other side.

Start out doing this Dancercize ten times, and work up to twenty times by sixty days.

RECREATION

Starting position 1. Sit on the floor with the bottoms of your feet together, knees bent. Keep your head tall, back straight and your arms out to the sides.
2. Keeping the same position, twist your upper body to the left.
3. Return to starting position and repeat to the other side.
Repeat this Dancercize ten times working up to twenty times within the next sixty days.

CIRCLE A

Starting position 1. Stand with legs slightly apart, round your arms in front of your body and circle your arms one over the other.
2. With one continuous flowing movement, begin to roll in a circle with your body.
3. Keep your arms circling.
4. Bend forward from the waist.
5. Roll your body at the waist to the left, with arms still circling.
6. Lean back from the waist.
7. Raise your arms above your head as your arms continue the rolling motion.
8. From the waist, roll to the right side.
9. Make ten circles with your body and then reverse the body cycle to the other side.
In sixty days you should be doing this Dancercize thirty times

PERPENDICULAR POLE

Starting position 1. Stand with legs apart and arms held rigid out to the sides.
2. Bend your left knee and lean a little to the left from your pelvis.
3. Extend your right arm up to the ceiling and your left hand rigid at the sides.
4. With a big stretch, lean from the waist all the way over to the right side, bending your right leg.
5. Raise your left arm up and back and touch the floor with your right fingertips.
6. Return to starting position, repeat to the left.

Repeat entire combination ten times. Work up to doing it twenty times within sixty days.

FINAL SUCCESS

Starting position 1. Kneel on floor. Bend your right leg back, and bend your left leg front with your left foot touching your right thigh.

2. Place your hands on the floor behind your back.

3. Keeping your arms straight behind your back, cross your right leg over your left leg and raise up on your left knee.

4. Keep head back.

5. Change legs and repeat to the other side.

Do this Dancercize five times.

HINDU STRETCH

Starting position 1. Sit on the floor, bend your left leg back.
2. Bend your right leg in so that your right toe touches your left thigh.
3. Raise up on your knees.
4. Stretch your arms above your head.
5. Bend back and stretch.
6. Turn the hands back to back fingers touching.
7. Lean to the left from the waist.
8. Lean to the right from your waist.
9. Return to starting position.

RIDE 'EM COWGIRL

Starting position 1. Sit on the floor with your legs drawn up to you.
2. Place the bottoms of your feet together.
3. Keep your back straight and head high.
4. Grab your ankles with your hands.
5. Keeping same position as above, open knees out and bounce, getting closer to the floor each time. Repeat this ten times to start, work up to twenty times within sixty days.

SASSY SIDE TWIST

Starting position 1. Sit on the floor bending your right leg back and your left knee front. Keep your body straight forward.

2. Turn your body and head to the left and *reach* out with your head and body as if someone was pulling you.

3. Return to starting position and repeat to the other side.

Repeat this Dancercize ten times, work up to twenty times within sixty days.

CAMERA THREE

Starting position 1. Stand tall and place your left foot behind your right, place your weight on your right leg.
2. Raise your arms above head.
3. Turn your body to the right as you raise your left knee as high as possible. Keep your arms above your head.
4. Keeping your body turned to the side, place your left leg on the floor—bent.
5. Keep your right leg straight and your weight on your left leg.
6. Repeat 3.
7. Return to starting position.
8. Repeat on the other side.
Do eight times to start with, work up to twenty within sixty days.

BEAUTIFULLY BOLD

Starting position 1. Sit on floor, bending your right leg back and your left knee front.
2. Hands on the floor behind your back.
3. Staying in the same position, raise up to your knees, pulling *forward* from your pelvis.
4. Remaining in the same position, raise your right arm above your head and twist your body to the left.
5. Return to picture No. 2, and raise your left arm above your head and twist your body to the right.
Repeat this Dancercize ten times to start, work up to twenty times in sixty days.

GRACEFUL STAND

Starting position 1. This Dancercize will teach you how to stand up from the floor gracefully. Sit on the floor and begin by bending your left leg in to your body.

2. Bend your right leg and keep your right foot on the floor.

3. Arms down, back straight and head elevated.

4. Push forward with your body with a thrust, until you come up on your right knee.

5. Try this four times.

6. Stand bent over, with your weight on your left leg.
7. Right (top of foot) foot resting behind your left foot on the floor.
8. Hands at your chest.

9. Begin to straighten your body.
10. Stand all the way up, bringing your arms up over your head. Turn your hands back to back and lean slightly back.
11. Now try the entire combination with the other leg. Repeat this Dancercize five times.

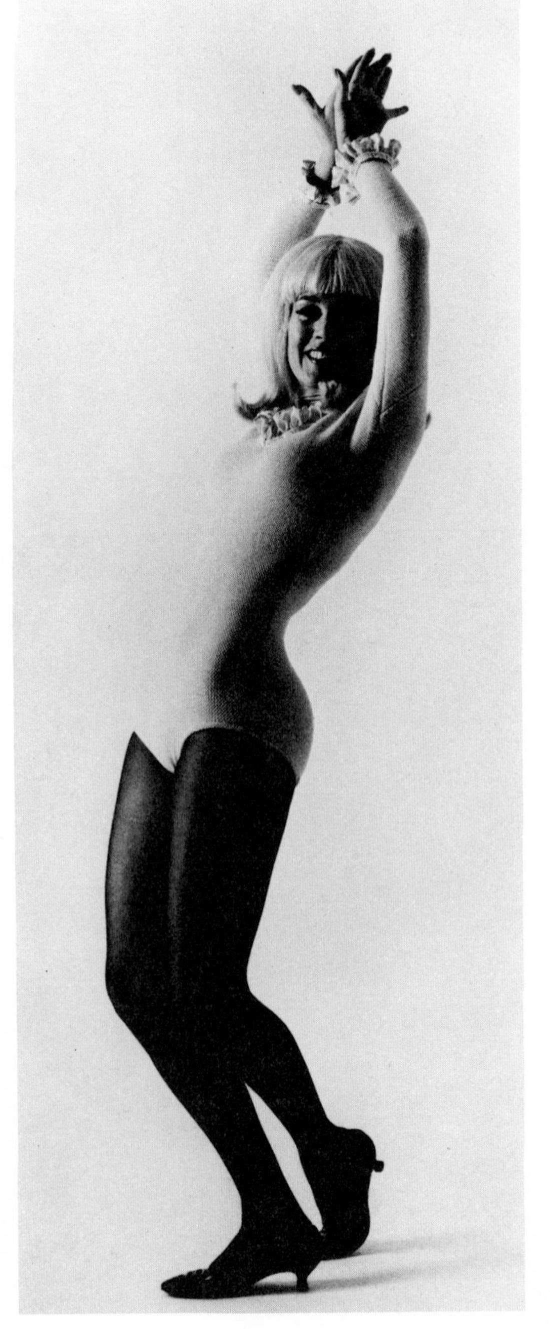

PLAYFUL

Starting position 1. Bend your left leg back and your right leg front.
2. Lean all the way over to the left side.
3. Raise your right arm up over your head and your left arm around your waist.
4. In the same position, raise up on your knees.
5. Raise all the way up on your knees, keeping your body front.
6. Place your left hand behind you on the floor and keep your right arm above your head.
7. Let your head go back.
8. Return to starting position, now reverse position and repeat other side. Repeat this Dancercize ten times, and work up to twenty within sixty days.

HINDU MOTION

Starting position 1. Stand with legs apart and body exalted. Place your hands at your chest keeping your elbows out.

2. Extend your right arm to the right side with index and thumb out (see illustration).

3. Lean to the right from the waist raising your right toe (heel on the floor) and bringing your right hand down to the toe.

4. Return to starting position.

5. Repeat to the left. Do this Dancercize ten times to the left and right alternately.
6. Now begin in the same starting position, but this time bring your leg and arm forward instead of to the side.
7. Repeat to the right, and do this alternating ten times.
8. Now, alternate entire combination. (Example: right side, left side, right front, left front.)
Have fun!

POLISHING THE PERSONALITY

Personality is like a gemstone. It may be polished to brilliance or left unfinished and rough. This chapter is designed to help make diamonds of coal. Among the facets of your personality are etiquette, conversation, sophistication, congeniality and sincerity.

Let us consider etiquette. Good etiquette is more than knowing which fork to use or how to introduce people to one another. It is the code by which we live as socially oriented human beings. Although certain rules of etiquette may vary with the times, the basics of civilized behavior remain unchanged. The purpose of these international rules is to aid us in establishing warm, personal relationships with our fellow man.

The three T's of good etiquette are Tact, Timing and Taste. To say what you think at the moment the thought is formed in a direct manner is *not* the key to popularity. Honesty is a virtue, particularly when combined with discretion. If a friend says to you, "I just love this dress, don't you?", she is usually asking for a confirmation, not for your true opinion. Even if you think the dress unbecoming, try to find something kind to say. Perhaps you might say, "The color is lovely" or "It is certainly the latest style." You are not being dishonest in a situation that clearly calls for tact. Whenever the need arises for you to criticize, be sure to remember this important T.

I was at the home of a friend recently when her young daughter asked for help with an English assignment. The girl showed her mother what she had done. Instead of saying, "No, that's all wrong", my friend wisely and tactfully complimented the child on her efforts and then went on to point out how the paper might be made better. Her material reward was gratitude rather than rebellion. This gift works as well with adults. A compliment first sweetens the criticism.

Correct timing is as important as tact. In the illustration above, if my friend had insisted on helping before her help was solicited, or if she had waited until the child's thoughts were wrapped up in another subject, her criticism would certainly have been less welcome, no matter how tactfully she phrased it. OFFER HELP ONLY WHEN IT IS WANTED. "Act (or speak) in haste and repent at leisure" is a motto worth remembering. Learn to take the time to consider the effect of your words or actions. Develop a good sense of timing. A man may laugh tomorrow at something that he is extremely sensitive about today.

Then again, he may not think it funny at all. This is where the third T comes in. Good taste will keep you from speaking of things that are offensive to others. Taste is also a guidepost to your appearance and actions. Dressing tastefully may not necessarily mean complying with the latest fad. If you are going to an afternoon tea, you would not want to appear with your hair piled three feet above your head. DRESS FOR THE OCCASION. Your actions are a good indication of your T.Q. (taste quotient). The other evening I attended a formal dinner party at which one of the guests spent the evening trying to be the "life of the party." He did everything but put a lampshade on his head. The other guests were bored or embarrassed, and an otherwise charming evening was ruined. Had the party been an informal one, his antics might have been considered amusing. SUIT YOUR ACTIONS TO THE OCCASION.

Your conversation is the window of your mind, through which your personality can be seen. If you wish to display a diamond rather than a lump of coal, see to it that your conversation is enthusiastic, yet brief and to the point. Show an interest in what others have to say and be tolerant of their ideas. Be willing to learn and ask intelligent questions which draw the other person out. Most of all, *be natural!* If you haven't been invited out lately, take a second look at your conversation.

How often do you use any of the personal pronouns (I, me, my, mine, myself)? Try talking for five minutes without using any of them.

Are you in love with the sound of your own voice? Interrupting and repeating yourself are a sure way to conversational suicide.

Do you argue or discuss? Discussion is an exchange of ideas. An argument is the exchange of words.

Do you talk down to people and pretend to know all the answers? Nothing is more boring than a "know-it-all." A superior attitude is not the mark of sophistication.

In our modern society, sophistication is often confused with pomposity. Pseudo-intellectualism is not worldly-wisdom. The society girl who has been sheltered by finishing schools is far more sophisticated, despite her pretension. Merriam-Webster defines sophistication as, "Of persons made wise . . . by experience." The truly sophisticated woman is charming, gracious, intelligent, glamorous, well-read and kind to animals, because experience has taught her that this is the best way to get along with people.

Congeniality is a vital component for a sparkling personality. As a polished stone picks up and reflects the colors that surround it, a woman should be able to mix with and adjust her personality to those around her. As an illustration of this, look at one of the TV personalities who acts as a master of ceremonies. He must be able to talk interestingly with athletes and statesmen, movie stars and authors, people from widely varied walks of life. DON'T LIMIT YOURSELF TO ONE SOCIAL OR ECONOMIC GROUP. When you find yourself among people whose ideas differ from yours, listen to their conversation and ask questions until you find some point of mutual interest. Your sincere desire to become a part of the group will overcome most barriers. Sincerity must come from within. You may learn etiquette and the art of conversation from books, you may gain sophistication and congeniality through experience, but all of these are merely surface without sincerity. A polished stone is worthless if there is an interior flaw. *Is insincerity the flaw in your personality?*

Many people have daily contact with women and work closely with them. Through their experiences, they are able to gain an insight into the female personality. Virginia Graham, of "Girl Talk," has a wonderful sense of perception of what women are really like. She is able to coordinate widely different personalities in an interesting and diplomatic manner. I asked her to give me a list of the personality traits she considers most important.

1. Warmth is the best gift.
2. Be compassionate.
3. Know when to be honest.
4. Give others credit for being intelligent.
5. Be interested in others, even if you have to force yourself.
6. Know when not to ask a question.
7. Do not be so eager to talk that you are not able to listen.
8. Anyone who sits in a corner and does not appear interested is not considered shy, but rude.

Dee Ellison, an outstanding hair stylist, had some very interesting comments on different types of women. She has the ability to put people at ease, and this, combined with a woman's natural affinity to talk to her hairdresser, qualifies her as one worth listening to. She places women in two classifications: Originals and Copies.

An Original
- looks as though she has just stepped out of Town & Country.
- is quiet and ladylike.
- never violates a confidence.
- respects her hair stylist as an artist.
- works with her hair so that she can give her stylist tips.
- gives her stylist the liberty to be creative, as long as she works within these tips.

A Copy
- must have the fad of the season, regardless of how it looks.
- has little or no regard for the next customer.
- orders people around.

She added that most women live in a small world and the only way to broaden that world is by an increased vocabulary. You only think with words you use. Too many times we adopt the opinion of one we respect or admire. Try to form sincere opinions rather than relying on stolen ones.

Then, in order to get the male point of view, I asked the public relations director of a large company to give me his opinion. I chose him because he has so much charm and finesse. He always dresses immaculately and is a diplomat in the true sense of the word. He, too, has the wonderful ability to put people at ease. Girls, if you would be attractive to men, pay particular attention to the following:

1. Men hate bossy women.
2. There is no justifiable reason for a woman to be slovenly.
3. Never put makeup on in public.
4. Men want femininity in a woman—not a "buddy."
5. Give all your attention to the person you are with.
6. Never leave your escort to visit with others—even on business.
7. Do not stop to visit on the way to or from the powder room.
8. Never laugh or speak in a loud manner.
9. Profanity is not attractive.
10. Do not appear overly-affectionate in public.

11. Be properly dressed for the occasion.
12. Act formally at a formal occasion—notice what is going on around you.
13. In ordering dinner, ask your date to make suggestions.
14. Never complain about the table, food, service, etc.
15. Never *tell* your escort to ask for a booth. You may make a suggestion, such as, "Wouldn't it be nice to have a booth?"
16. Do not make unreasonable or selfish demands.

Perhaps some of the ideas presented here are new to you. I'm sure that many of them are familiar. Use this chapter as a measuring stick for *your* personality, and if you find some of the suggestions difficult to follow, don't let yourself become discouraged. Even though it might not come naturally first, it will become easier as you concentrate on improving yourself. Read books—work at it, but don't follow the rules for the sake of the rules alone. Put yourself in the other person's place and you will be able to see the reason behind each rule. Remember, the rules only serve as a guide toward a happier, more satisfying life.

BEAUTY IS MORE THAN A FIGURE AND FACE

In previous generations a woman's charm could easily be seen because it was usually visual. A lithe figure and a winsome smile were once a woman's principal assets. The only conversation expected of her concerned family and home. Much more is expected of the modern woman. Because of the improved standards of education, women's horizons have expanded. Self-development should be the key to every woman's personality. A rounded education, often denied her by the masculine world of fifty years ago, now enables her to touch life at many points.

Culture, literature, drama, music, art and the social sciences are the crystallization of man's efforts to understand himself.

Over the centuries the most perceptive thinkers have compiled a bibliography of their personal visions, and this reservoir of thought and perception can enrich your existence. You can draw on the best in the arts and social sciences to shape your life.

Why is this chapter important to you? Mainly because physical beauty isn't enough. The respect of others is definitely important, but the true meaning of cultural awareness must lie on a more personal level. Even if those around you don't suspect your shallowness, it can trigger within you a personal sense of insecurity. Most important, though, knowledge illuminates your own life besides giving you mere social ease. This personal search for wider horizons is the essence of growth. Through deep self-understanding, you are in a position to understand those around you, both as a social group and as individuals. This result will help you become a more rounded individual.

THE WORLD OF BOOKS

Here are a few suggestions on books to introduce you to the world of the writer.

One of the most readable of American authors is Nobel Prize winner Pearl Buck. Her concern is with people as individuals. Her style is readable, and her subject matter is interesting, especially since much of it deals with China, the land in which she was raised and whose language she spoke even before English. *The Good Earth*, her best known novel, is the story of a Chinese peasant's rise from poverty to riches with the help of his faithful wife. The suffering of the peasant's family and the unfailing loyalty of his wife, who continues to love him even after he takes a mistress, are memorable. Though set in a foreign land with unfamiliar people and customs, *The Good Earth* has universal appeal because it is concerned with human values which can be translated into any language.

To those who like the story of the Southwest without the brutality of television westerns, Willa Cather provides a perceptive study of rural folk in her romantic novels. Her best known novel, *Death Comes for the Archbishop*, tells the story of a young, sensitive, intellectual priest's struggle to civilize the rugged New Mexico frontier. The straightforward, optimistic tone of the book combined with the exotic, historical mood makes this Cather's most memorable work.

The goal of all short-story writers is to say the most in the least number of words. A master of concision is Anton Chekhov. His short, sympathetic stories of the poor in Russia reflect extreme sensitivity and compassion, but still remain terse and objective. Two of his very short and very tragic stories are "Heartache," an old man's unsuccessful search for sympathy, and "Christmas Time," a moving tale of human misunderstanding. Chekhov's concern is with life as it is visible in his characters. Like many Russian authors he philosophizes through story telling.

Fortunately for the modern reader, Feodor Dostoevski, the long-winded Russian author, wrote a novelette, titled *Notes from Underground*. Dostoevski's ideas are complex and often tempt the reader to give up in frustration. His witty style, however, gives life to the character who is supposedly writing the *Notes*, which makes even the reading difficulties pleasurable. From the opening lines, "I'm a sick man . . . a mean man, there's nothing attractive about me. I think there's something wrong with my liver," passing through his comic affair with a local prostitute, to the ending which abruptly drops off because the supposed author is tired of writing the book, the *Notes From Underground* is humorous and fascinating. To read it is to discipline the mind.

Stephen Crane, the tragic young American author, led a life as exciting and doomed as his writings. Crane is concerned with the problems of man as a part of society. He deals with universal problems of mankind, such as war in the *Red Badge of Courage*, and the indifference of fate in the *Open Boat*. But his primary concern is with social injustice, as explored in his novelette *Maggie, A Girl of the Streets*. Crane is perhaps the first American novelist to deal with the important problems of alcoholism, prostitution and slums. He is at the same time a master of concise, beautiful imagery and extremely sensitive to nature. His novel *Maggie, A Girl of the Streets*, though it champions Maggie's innate virtue, was considered shocking because its subject, prostitution, was one to be ignored, not resolved, in its time.

Like Stephen Crane, F. Scott Fitzgerald was also concerned with social disease, but at the opposite end of the social scale. His characters, the drifting social elite seeking real moral values upon which to base their lives, would be equally at home in our world as in Fitzgerald's Twenties. Perhaps the most characteristic view of the fragile society of the rich is in his novel *Tender Is the Night*, a story of a brilliant psychiatrist who marries a former patient and then is lured to a dissolute life on the French Riviera. Fitzgerald stresses the importance of idealism by showing characters who frantically but unsuccessfully strive for it.

The sense of loss that typifies *Tender Is the Night* is central to *The Sun Also Rises* by the Nobel Prize winner, Ernest Hemingway. Both novels show the "lost generation" of the Twenties, a generation whose ambition and idealism were destroyed by World War I.

Often an author's own life as well as his ideas are used as material for a novel. *Of Human Bondage*, by Somerset Maugham, is the story of a young man in search of his personality and calling in life. Much of the story is taken from the author's own life. The central character is an impoverished medical student who is torn between love for an unresponsive woman and idealism. This book has provided the basis for an extremely popular movie.

"The things I have written of in this memoir are very close to my heart." This closing line from James Michener's best selling novel *Hawaii* is an accurate summary of all his writings. He writes of thousands of small experiences, both real and imaginatively reconstructed, which have grown to maturity in his fertile mind, to produce novels filled with thousands of photographically clear, artfully colored scenes. Such novels as *Hawaii* are rich in interesting people and colorful experiences which paint a vivid panorama of places and events.

Upon opening the pages of a book of John O'Hara, the reader is violently injected into a social rat race, a world of the socially sick seeking "life." The environment of his novel *A Rage to Live* is one torn by emptiness, an environment which the main character has no control over, for she is the product of a society which cripples her every action. Mr. O'Hara has often been accused of being a dirty writer, but according to a recent Supreme Court decision, a work may not be considered pornographic if it has redeeming social values.

Katherine Ann Porter quickly establishes a mood, usually an exotic mood. The talent for establishment of mood is essential to all short-story writers, but Miss Porter has developed it into a fine art—depicting in her story "Rope," the emotional relationship between a man and a woman with little more than dialogue. Her choices of characters and settings are extremely unusual. Her simple, fluid style can convey an extremely subtle meaning or a broad general story depending on the reader's effort. She is rewarding on almost any level. Some of her best stories include *Flowering Judas*, "Rope," "Maria Concepcion" and "The Jilting of Grannie Weatherall."

Perhaps the novelist Ayn Rand's great contribution to letters is that she forces readers to define more clearly their own views. She lives by the philosophy that is expressed in *Atlas Shrugged* and neither wants to nor expects to depend on the help of others. She believes that if one accepts helping others as good, and self-interest as bad, then one enslaves himself. She replaces the time-honored morality of helping others with a morality of "rational self-interest." Reason becomes the way of survival not for others but for oneself.

Out of the American depression of the 1930's arose a new social consciousness. This consciousness, based upon a more vivid and personal contact with poverty, broke to the literary surface in the torrent of John Steinbeck. The delicate balance between poignant beauty and startling ugliness is resolved in his short novel of *Of Mice and Men*. Steinbeck's storytelling powers reached their height in *East of Eden*, a modern adaptation of the Biblical story of Cain and Abel reset in Southern California. Steinbeck is able to portray characters who are real people and at the same time symbolic figures. His sense of social consciousness and excellent writing were responsible for his Nobel Prize award.

J.R.R.Tolkien, the modern English novelist, has created one of the most fascinating epics since Homer in *The Lord of the Rings*. His basic simplicity of style makes the three-book cycle purely enjoyable. Any description of the plot would sound ridiculous; the books must be read for appreciation of their charm and enchantment. Although the characters are mythological hobbits, elves, dwarves, ents; Tolkien's clear understanding of human nature makes even the absurd seem real. The reader never feels as if she is reading a fairy tale, but rather a sometimes humorous and sometimes moving tale told from a great imagination.

Made even more popular by the fact that he was President Kennedy's acknowledged poet, Robert Frost was often characterized as a kindly old man who wrote only such sentimental poems as "Stopping by the Woods on a Snowy Evening." This role, however, is really too limited, for even "Stopping by Woods" is more than a sentimental old man's reflections, and such poems as "Nothing Gold Can Stay" sound a much less sentimental chord. His resourceful depictions of nature and thought alike are indicative of his versatility and intellect.

Kahlil Gibran has been a favorite of the past two generations largely because of his long narrative poem *The Prophet*. His simple direct style heightened with poetic beauty makes this mystical poem an expression of intellectual and emotional impulses. The poem is one of the reasons that Gibran is often referred to as a philosopher, for it represents his views on subjects ranging from love to death.

Though a fairly modern American poet, Edna St. Vincent Millay is often compared with nineteenth-century English romantic poets. This comparison is a tribute to her ability to write beautiful, regular, but still intellectual verse. Her best known poem, *Renascence,* written in 1911 at the age of nineteen, is a magnificent questioning of life.

If you want to impress a man with your appreciation of poetry and at the same time want him to enjoy sharing it, be sure to find something he will like. While Frost seems popular with both men and women, and Cummings appeals to both, many poets are strongly preferred by only one sex. Edgar Lee Master's *Spoon River Anthology,* a rather realistic collection of short poems about the dead of a small town, might be appropriate for a man with a strong sense of irony. Another good poet with similar inclinations is Edward Arlington Robinson whose *Town Down the River* is much like *Spoon River;* his famed poem *Richard Cory* will certainly be long remembered.

To grasp the subtleties of Shakespeare, there are several things you should do: first, read a short plot summary before seeing the play, making sure you know the characters (and the murders in a tragedy); second, don't worry if the language doesn't make sense at first, because if you know the basic story, it will become easier to understand the lines as the play progresses.

If you are serious about wanting to broaden your interest and knowledge in literature—if you want to read for education as well as pleasure—you might go to your local library for guidance. Incidentally, it is a good idea to read within a period. For instance, if you want to know about life in the Twenties, you can go beyond Fitzgerald and Hemingway to Dreiser and Cabell and other writers. One suggestion that I have found helpful. When I was listening to Straus' Waltzes, I found myself very curious about life in Austria during the period Straus was composing, and so I read books on the Royal Family, and the combination of music and books made the times come alive to me. The suggestions in this chapter are not meant to substitute for any courses in reading on art, history, or music. They have helped me and I pass them along as helpful hints to you.

Much more concerned with society than with people themselves are Tennessee Williams and Arthur Miller. They both stress realism to the utmost even though it may at times be harsh or obscene (as in Williams' case). In Williams' famous *Cat on a Hot Tin Roof*, a few of man's basic problems (death, cancer, alcoholism, homosexuality, sexual frustration, greed . . .) are considered. Arthur Miller's *The Crucible* is also a naturalistic drama of human passion. Set in Puritan New England, it shows how hatred and jealousy can blind man. More specifically, a spiteful young girl is able to have innocent women executed as witches through her amoral cunning and sexual attractiveness.

Eugene O'Neill is often said to be the greatest playwright America has produced to date. The largely autobiographical and extremely intimate *Long Day's Journey* relates the events of a single day in a family much like O'Neill's own. In fact, the play was so personal that it was withheld from publication until after his death. The younger of the two sons, Edmund, who is supposed to be modeled after O'Neill himself, is a sensitive, would-be writer who is dying of tuberculosis because of his father's thrift in selecting a doctor. Mary, the mother, is an intermittently insane morphine addict also because of the father's greed. Jamey, the eldest son, is a drunk who constantly criticizes the father. Tyrone, the father, is a flamboyant, selfish individual.

One of the brightest lights in America's younger generations of playwrights is Edward Albee, whose dramatic expression has brought him to the forefront. The power of his drama rests in the savage realism of his dialogue and the brutal theme of frustrated human desire. His characters rend themselves viciously in their attempts to penetrate each others walls of fear and self-doubt. Two of his plays which center on this vital theme of human misunderstanding are *The Zoo Story,* a short one-act play, and *Who's Afraid of Virginia Woolf,* which has been made into a successful movie.

The themes of Albee reflect a new movement in the field of drama—the "Theater of the Absurd." The playwrights dealing with this form have one basic objective in mind, and that is to present the absurdity of the human situation. The presentation is at times funny and at times sad. The play seems to lose all touch with reality, but in the end the absurd becomes sad actuality. Ionesco's first play, or "antiplay" as he terms it, *The Bald Soprano,* represents the basic elements of the Theater of the Absurd. The characters speak as thought they are not aware of the existence of those around them. They often act as if they did not even hear the other person's dialogue. Even within the context of a single person's dialogue there is often no continuity or semblance of sense; actions are often meaningless as a character goes offstage to change clothes and reenters in the exact same wardrobe. In short, the Theater of the Absurd is a parody, a rejection of the existence of all sense and continuity in modern life.

When you go to the theater, you will find it rewarding to know something of a play's history. It will intensify your pleasure in the play and give you the self-assurance so necessary to poise. However, don't belabor the point. Never allow your escort to be put in the dubious position of feeling you are his intellectual superior. Men, poor dears, simply can't take it. This capsule of information on books, drama and art is for *your* benefit and only by indirection for his.

HOW DO YOU LEARN TO ENJOY MUSIC?

The choice of your tune, whether it be a Mozart sonata or a Beatles' song, depends on your feelings, because music is basically emotional. Nevertheless, the more you know about the technique of music, the greater will be your enjoyment. In spite of the academic mask which is often placed over music's face, it is probably the warmest and most openly emotional of all arts. The difference between the happy sounds of a child in his cradle and the polished gems of Beethoven is not basic, but rather a separation of degree, since both want primarily to express their emotions.

In spite of the fact that some of us may think symphonic music is boring, record companies have made money selling the "classics reclassified," to the public, as with the conversion of both a Tchaikovsky piano concerto and a Bach piano piece into popular hit records.

What you want is to learn enough of classical music so that you can find the pieces that will genuinely capture your interest. The basic guideline to classical music is period—as in art, classical music is divided into chronological periods with the pieces in a given period having general similarity. Perhaps the most interesting musical period for the girl who wants to learn the elementals is the Romantic period (early nineteenth to early twentieth centuries). The music of Romantic composers is appealing because of their open warmth. Thanks to the second of the three great B's (Bach, Beethoven and Brahms) music underwent a tremendous resurrection of emotional emphasis. Beethoven's rebellious personality caused him to experiment with new musical forms which produced powerful and beautiful sounds. Beethoven's drive was so strong that even when in old age he became totally deaf, he still created works like his *Ninth Symphony* which is written for a full chorus, soloists and orchestra. In addition, he wrote numerous concertos for piano and orchestra as well as a *Violin Concerto*.

The new romantic temperament flavored by Russian tradition produced such passionate works as Tchaikovsky's *Fifth Symphony, Piano Concerto, Violin Concerto,* and the musical fantasy *Romeo and Juliet*. Despite the scandalous life led by Franz Liszt (or perhaps because of it) his piano concerto and his tone poem *Les Preludes* are among the most emotional and impressive of the entire Romantic Period. An admirer of Beethoven, Brahms created four original symphonies containing some of the most beautiful of all melodies.

More unusual in their musical styles are Nikolai Rimski-Korsakov and Gustav Mahler. The exotic quality of Rimski-Korsakov's *Scheherazade,* whose story was drawn from the mystic *Arabian Nights,* carries the listener through vivid throes of passion. The ten symphonies of Mahler are self-portraits of emotion in their tracing of the psychological torments and eventual breakdown of the man.

More melodic and contemporary are the works of Ralph Vaughan Williams and Aaron Copland who are nationalistic in their use of native folk melodies. Vaughan Williams was able to adapt traditional English themes, such as his *Fantasia on a Theme of Greensleeves*. Aaron Copland's earlier works, *Appalachian Spring* and *Billy the Kid,* make pastoral America come alive in the simplicity of their folk beauty.

Now that you know something about symphonic music (which is music for listening), it's time to talk about opera (which is music for watching). As in television, however, the audio portion of opera is still important if for no other reason than to explain the visual. From the light, gay stories of

Rossini's *Barber of Seville* and Mozart's *Marriage of Figaro* to the more serious stories of Puccini's *Madame Butterfly* and *La Boheme* to Verdi's *Rigoletto* and *Aida*, opera provides an entertaining, compelling narrative as well as magnificent music. If the opera is to be sung in Italian, you should read a plot summary ahead of time. Even if the opera is in English, it is still a good idea to read a plot summary before the performance so that you may concentrate fully on the musical splendor of the opera.

Incidentally, you don't need much money to enjoy music. A record player is necessary. And a card to the local library. Many public libraries have excellent record libraries which loan or rent (at a very small fee) records of their patrons.

NOW FOR THE BALLET

Ballet dancing is the highly developed and polished art of interpreting music through bodily movement. The dance is a pantomime expression of the composer's music.

ART

The Renaissance period in fifteenth century Italy was marked by great activity in many fields including art, science, music, philosophy, and sex (remember this is the birth of humanism). This flurry of activity is supposed to have centered around a rediscovery of Greek and Roman art and literature. In painting and sculpture this new concern reflected itself in the human more than the abstract.

It is by use of light that Masaccio, for example, gave a sense of depth to his paintings which was largely lacking in the work of his predecessors. In addition Masaccio used color effectively. It is this use of color in *Expulsion From Paradise* which emphasizes the anguish on the faces of Adam and Eve as they sorrowfully leave the Garden of Eden.

Even as early as the time of Sandro Botticelli (1444-1491), men were acutely aware of a woman's body, although Botticelli's sensual idealization of the female nude, as in his *Birth of Venus*, may seem a trifle hefty to the modern woman.

In contrast to the Spanish system and previous medieval systems under which the Church had been the sole patron, sensual painting was fairly common in renaissance Italy due, no doubt, to the abundance of lecherous patrons.

Leonardo da Vinci (1452-1519) was a genius whose studies of the human body were fantastically scientific. Leonardo painted extremely accurate and beautiful pictures of the human body. His most famous painting is of course the *Mona Lisa.* One of the great tragedies is that Leonardo, through his innate genius, accidentally destroyed some of his best work. His famous painting, *The Last Supper,* during his own lifetime started flaking off the wall on which it was painted, because he used experimental techniques in making it.

In sculpture, Michaelangelo's statues have perhaps the most lifelike bodies in all of art. Even the hands of his *David,* in the swelling of delicate muscles, show the extreme tension David felt in facing the giant Goliath. Though primarily a sculptor, Michelangelo was extremely versatile, working as a sculptor, painter, architect, and sometimes even a poet. Nonetheless, it is as a sculptor that his reknown is the greatest; it has been said that many sculptors regretted his having lived in that he left nothing to surpass for those who followed him.

Peter Paul Rubens (1577-1640), almost always painted robust and heroic women. The vivid colors and frame-overflowing pictures of voluptuous bodies are typical of his period, the Baroque. The height of his sensuality is shown in the masterpiece *Diana Returning From the Hunt.*

One of Rembrandt Von Riijn's (1606-1669) spell-binding pictures is *The Binding of Samson.* Rembrandt is renowned chiefly for his sensitive portrayal of facial expression; though he may have a half a dozen or more characters in a painting, each remains a distinct individual.

One of the so-called fathers of "Impressionism," Claude Monet (1840-1926) failed to make much of an impression on the early art critics, so they insulted him by inventing the word "impressionism" to describe his painting *Impression—Sunrise.* As the art critics stepped back from the pastel painting in time and space, they found that the curious patches of paint began to merge into a picture, and a new bright light was born. The pastel beauty of the light, lyrical paintings of Monet represent a true picture of the painter's immediate impression of the landscape before him. He captured one view of the *River* in which the sun was so bright that certain critics claimed that it hurt their eyes.

Reacting against Monet's impressionism, Paul Cezanne (1840-1926) produced a union of the styles of Rembrandt and Monet. That is, he liked the basic idea of impressionism—subjective impressions of landscapes, but he felt they lacked the substantial form and structure of the old Dutch masters, particularly Rembrandt. He tried to harmonize these values in his own scheme of painting which strove for a philosophical interpretation of essential reality. That is, what he paints may not look like what it is but rather what it really is (to him); hence, by this union he became the "Father of Modern Art."

Pablo Picasso is perhaps the greatest of the modern artists. Picasso started with the traditional (in this case Spanish) and sought an ultimate vision of reality through constant experiments. In Picasso's Blue Period, all of his people were blue, both emotionally and physically. Putting on rose-colored glasses, he climaxed his next period with *Gertrude Stein*. This painting, during his Rose Period, was greatly influenced by primitive African sculpture. Picasso launched the cubist movement which emphasized geometrical forms and was based on an idea pioneered by Cezanne—overlapping several different views of the same object to add a fourth dimension to painting, that of time. This was merely another attempt to discover essential reality at the expense of mere appearance. A good example of this period is the *Accordionist*. One of his great paintings, *Guernica*, is a surrealistic cry against totalitarianism in its picture of the horrors of the bombing of the city Guernica during the Spanish Civil War. This striking painting is intended as an expression of Picasso's belief in the supreme worth of the individual.

The latest generation of artists started "Pop Art." The five men instrumental in the creation of pop art are Roy Lichtenstein, Claes Oldenburg, James Rosenquist, Andy Warhol and Tom Wesselman. Their individual concepts of art vary widely, but they all work through the medium of familiar objects of our daily life. These objects include such normally non-artistic items as "Little Orphan Annie" comic strips, *Time* magazine covers and chicken soup cans. The intent of pop art varies greatly with the artist.

One artist sees a crumpled gum wrapper as pure poetic form, while another will exploit its tremendous value as social commentary. Holding at least alphabetical precedence over pop art is "Op Art." Op art depends upon the natural imperfections of the eye to create amazing effects which range from seeing apparent motion and color in still black lines, to mistaking straight lines for curved ones.

From the psychologist's abnormal interest in your scribbling to the sociologist's pathological love for back-alley trash cans, scientists are continually prying into the most seemingly insignificant aspects of your life. Our society depends upon these scientists to inform it of its needs. While the fine arts portray literature, drama, music, and art, the scientist systematically dissects them. The fine arts attempt to communicate directly with the audience without explaining things much—they merely show you their subject and expect you to work out some sort of reaction to it. The scientist's whole job is to figure out and explain the objects of your life to you.

The behavioral psychologist believes that all behavior is a product of conditioning—that is, that an individual can be trained to respond exactly as her controller desires, provided that the conditioning technique is correct and the basic actions are within the subject's capacity. This theory says that all so-called "natural" behavior in the individual is a result of unconscious daily conditioning which affects all people from the time of their birth. The behavioral psychologist usually bases his theories on experimental evidence. One of the best known examples of the conditioning principle is the experiment of Pavlov's dogs. Pavlov rang a small bell before feeding his dogs. He repeated this process over and over until the dogs had associated the bell with food. Then to test his theory he rang withe bell *without* feeding them, and they still drooled. Since no such reaction was observed in dogs not bell broken, it seemed clear that the dogs had associated the bell with food.

A much more traditional means of analyzing people is Freudian psychology. This concept was named after its founder Sigmund Freud. Rather then running extensive statistical tests to evaluate his complexes, Freud almost always tried to theorize existing behavior in terms of a subject's early life. He divided this early life into a series of traditional phases which were supposed to come in a set order, and the resulting personality would be due to the intensity of the various phases. Freud also believed that most abnormal behavior was the result of a conflict between repressed desire and the conscious will which, out of guilt, repressed the desire. This theory applies mainly to sex.

Regardless of how you approach psychology, the basic aim is the same; all psychologists are analyzing the individual—that is, the "self" and how it works. No matter what sort of approach a psychologist takes, whether it is experimenting with chickens and dogs or dividing a child's life into phases, he is merely trying to order the process of self-understanding. As a science, psychology is an unemotional way to further your self-understanding, *perhaps the most important goal in life.* Not only is this self-understanding personally beneficial, but when you have achieved a degree of self-understanding, you can better understand those around you.

Now if you can get together at someone's house with friends and try to analyze each other, two interesting things will happen, both of which will lead you to the entrance of sociology. First, you will quickly note that there are a lot of similarities among the ideas you and your friends have. But if you invite someone in from a different part of town or a different background, you may be amazed at the difference. This similarity among people with common ties of education and income level makes the socio-economic groups of our society.

Of course, sociologists could usually tell you more than this. They can even tell you more about yourself because they know you as a part of a larger group, namely, your society. By being aware of the group forces—income, religion, ethnic group, education and a multitude of others—you can isolate many of the personal characteristics which have come to you from your contact with society. In the same way, you can see how these forces affect the people around you. Ultimately, you should be able to see how they work on your entire society, affecting such things as government, fashions and, of course, the average man's concept of the ideal woman.

If you want to expand your horizons, here is a reading list that may be helpful.

POETRY

Sound and Sense, by Laurence Perrine. A basic textbook explaining the basic forms and techniques of poetry with extremely well chosen examples.

How Does a Poem Mean, by John Ciardi. A discussion of the more artistic aspects of poetry written by a talented contemporary poet.

DRAMA

The Living Theater, by Elmer Rice. A general discussion of the history and origins of modern American theater.

The Theater of the Absurd, by Martin Easlin. A discussion of the intent of the modern Theater of the Absurd made clear by specific treatment of its playwrights and plays.

The Living Stage: A History of the World Theater, by Kenneth MacGowan and William Melnitz. Offers a panoramic view of the ever-changing world theater.

The Play and the Reader, by Stanley Johnson, Judah Bierman and James Hart. An introduction to drama designed to show how a dramatist uses different forms and techniques to present his view of life.

MUSIC

Discovering Music, by Howard McKinney. A presentation of useful techniques for listening to and understanding music.

An Introduction to Music, 3rd Edition by Martin Bernstein and Martin Picker. Covers the principal periods in the development of music including analyses of works representative of the major forms and composers.

Music Lover's Encyclopedia, by Rupert Hughes. A categorized listing of musical terminology, composers, and famous pieces which will clarify confusion on musical topics.

In addition, one of the most rewarding and easiest ways to gradually learn about music is simply by reading the backs of record jackets.

ART

History of Art, by H. W. Janson. A definitive treatment of the major periods in art, using many excellent black and white and color plates.

Art Through the Ages, by Helen Gardner. Another excellent overall history of art.

A Concise History of Modern Painting, by Herbert Read. A thorough but brief survey of the schools of modern art.

Sight and Insight, by Alexander Eliot. A well written book which teaches good attitudes for the fullest enjoyment of art.

Art as Image and Idea, by Edmund B. Feldman. Presents an analysis of art in terms of its function, styles, structure, techniques and relations to society.

There are also several inexpensive paperback collections of reproductions of famous artists with excellent critical commentary.

PSYCHOLOGY

Basic Teachings of Great Psychologists, by S. Stansfeld Sargent. A readable review of the classical approaches to psychology.

Readings in General Psychology, ed. Lester Crow. A collection of important writings on different aspects of psychology.

Walden II, by B. F. Skinner. A thought-provoking novel which extends behaviorist theory to its ultimate implications.

Sex and the Office, by Helen Gurley Brown. Useful tips on how to use the office for your own advantage.

Woman, by Dr. Joyce Brothers. A sensitive examination of the emotional problems faced by the modern woman.

How to Win Friends and Influence People, by Dale Carnegie. A practical book on good human relations.

Loneliness, by Clarke E. Moustakas. Explores beauty and terror in loneliness as revealed in personal documents and poems and the lives of solitary individuals.

Understanding Ourselves and Others, by Kurt Haas. Contains information provided by psychologists, psychiatrists and other scientists so that readers may better understand themselves and intelligently perceive the behavior of others.

The Dynamics of Personal Adjustment, by George F. J. Lehner and Ella Kube. Presents the person in society, stressing the adjustment problems we all face as a continuing learning process.

SOCIOLOGY

The Lonely Crowd, by David Riesman. A general survey of sociological concepts and techniques.

Status Seekers, by Vance Packard. An interesting collection of surprising and enlightening facts about modern American society.

White Collar, by C. Mills. A more detailed analysis of the so-called "white collar" stratum of our society.

ASTROLOGY

Astrology, by Louis MacNeice. Persuasive arguments in favor of astrology complete with the history, techniques and examples of astrology.

PHRENOLOGY

How to Read Character: New Illustrated Handbook of Phrenology and Physiognomy for Students and Examiners with a Descriptive Chart. A rather quaint manual on the practical applications of phrenology written in the heyday of the science. This is a fun book.

Phrenology: Fad and Science, by John Davies. A more critical analysis of phrenology.

ANTHROPOLOGY

Sex and Temperament, by Margaret Mead. A book trying to show that masculine and feminine behavior are determined by social attitude rather than sex.

African Genesis, by Robert Ardrey. A startling but carefully presented theory on man's rise based on his capacity to kill.

MAGAZINES

Just as the usual groceries must be supplemented with daily vitamins, so must the basics of culture (books) be supplemented with smaller, more frequent boosts (magazines). News and fashion magazines provide current and essential sources of information that *every* social-minded girl should use.

U.S. News and World Report. A magazine which discusses a few of the most important news happenings in some depth.

Time. A quicker, less detailed skim of news events as well as critical analysis of plays, books and movies.

Newsweek. Similar to *Time* in its method and subject though much more liberal in its political slant.

Vogue. An up-to-date magazine showing the trends in the world of fashion.

Harper's Bazaar. Like *Vogue* in its subject, presenting what every social-minded girl should know.

Cosmopolitan. A more general magazine covering subjects from news to beauty tips, attempting to provide the modern woman with what she needs to know.

THE ART OF LIVING

Now you have almost finished reading my book. If you have gained even a small fragment of knowledge about how to get more living out of your life I will have been deeply rewarded for the effort that went into this book.

Before we part, via the printed page, I would like to leave one final thought with you. Your time on this glorious earth is merely an allotment. The sum of moments, months and years that is your life is merely on loan to you by your Creator. Almost everyone born on this earth is endowed with a certain amount of ability—even talent.

Often our talents and abilities are lying dormant like seeds in a garden, waiting only to be watered and nourished by desire in order to grow. And I am sure that God's greatest delight must come in seeing those persons who keep pressing beyond what seems like a minimum of equipment to accomplish their desires.

Dr. Paul Tournier, famous philosopher of our time, says that man does not die; he kills himself—through years of faulty diet, intemperance, boredom, and mental and moral conflicts that slowly erode his vitality.

Just as health is not merely an absence of the symptoms of illness, happiness is not just the absence of unhappiness. Happiness (and health) is a wholeness. Wholeness comes from an awareness of yourself and your relationship to the world around you.

It doesn't matter whether you live in an apartment or on a beach with crashing surf and rugged rocks. You are an integral part of the life around you, and with every breath you draw you are helping to forge the continuing chain of history.

What do you know about your state, your town or even the small segment of the community in which you live. Was it once an Indian campsite? Was it once used to graze cattle and sheep? Was it farmland that eventually evolved into a village, then a city?

Whose concern helped to develop a center of government, build a library, schools and churches? Every landmark represents people, aware people who cared about other people.

So let me urge you to take time each day to *look* at your world and *listen* with more awareness. If you think you are seeing and hearing everything, try taking a small child for a walk. You may be surprised at how much you have been missing.

There is happiness in small joys. There is beauty in a poem, a good book —there is also beauty in a line of clean wash, a trim lawn or flower bed.

Relax and listen to good music. But don't forget to listen to the symphony of nature: the wind in the treetops, bird songs, thundering surf. There is one kind of beauty in a rushing mountain stream, another in a quiet pool; and no canvas can equal any one of a week's sunsets, or the pink new world of dawn.

Listen with your heart. Try to hear what the other person is *saying*. Put yourself in his place and try to hear his problems as your own.

Tune your ears too, to hear love and hope and courage instead of gossip, malice and resentment. Keep your mind open to new ideas. Seek the truth; challenge assertions, ideas, and philosophies, and listen with patience to the other person even when you do not agree. You just might learn something.

And don't be afraid to show your ignorance. Ask questions. Almost everyone you come in contact with has something to say that will add to your mental growth.

But above all, listen to yourself—listen to your deepest desires, your noblest impulse or aspiration. Listen to that better person deep within you. Listen to and trust your feminine intuition—and know life abundantly.

Sincerely,

Debbie Drake